VIKING

The publishers gratefully acknowledge
assistance from Haslemere Estates and the Pension Fund
Property Unit Trust, which has covered the cost
of the gatefold sections in this book.

CLIVE ASLET

QUINLAN TERRY

The Revival of Architecture

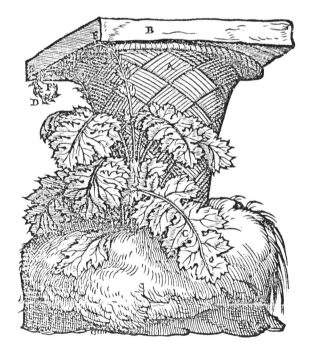

VIKING

VIKING

Penguin Books Ltd, Harmondsworth, Middlesex, England
Viking Penguin Inc., 40 West 23rd Street, New York,
New York 10010, U.S.A.
Penguin Books Australia Ltd, Ringwood, Victoria, Australia
Penguin Books Canada Limited, 2801 John Street, Markham,
Ontario, Canada L3R 1B4
Penguin Books (N.Z.) Ltd, 182–190 Wairau Road,
Auckland 10, New Zealand

First published 1986

Typeset in Linotype Galliard by
Wordsmiths Typesetting, Somerset
Printed in Great Britain by
Butler and Tanner Ltd
Frome, Somerset

British Library Cataloguing in Publication Data

Aslet, Clive
Quinlan Terry: the revival of architecture.
1. Terry, Quinlan   2. Architects—Biography
I. Title
720'.92'4   NA997.T/
ISBN 0–670–80831–8

The illustration on the title page is from
Giovanantonio Rusconi's *Della Architectura* (Venice, 1590).
It shows the origin of the Corinthian capital according to Vitruvius
(Book IV, Chapter 1): '… just then Callimachus passed by the tomb
and observed the basket with the tender young leaves growing
round it. Delighted with the novel style and form he built
some columns after the pattern for the Corinthians.'
Quinlan Terry's ideas about the origin of the orders
are set out in Chapter 11.

CONTENTS

TO MY FATHER

LIST OF FIGURES

LIST OF FIGURES

LIST OF FIGURES

LIST OF FIGURES

LIST OF FIGURES

ARCHITECTURE has its political Use; publick Buildings being the Ornament of a Country; it establishes a Nation, draws People and Commerce; makes the People love their native Country, which Passion is the Original of all great Actions in a Commonwealth. The Emulation of the Cities of *Greece* was the true Cause of their Greatness. The obstinate Valour of the *Jews*, occasioned by the Love of their Temple, was a Cement that held together that People, for many Ages, through infinite Changes …

Architecture aims at Eternity; and therefore the only Thing uncapable of Modes and Fashions in its Principals, the *Orders*.

SIR CHRISTOPHER WREN, *Parentalia*

PREFACE

In 1962, when Quinlan Terry went to work with Raymond Erith in rural Dedham, it may have seemed that his professional existence would be spent in a kind of exile. He had exchanged the hard, profit-dominated world of architecture in London for a world in which he would be true to his principles, but perhaps largely doomed to supervising country-house extensions and roof repairs in the neighbouring villages of East Anglia. The extensions and repairs would have been beautifully conceived and ably executed. But they would not have given the scope that offices, universities and public buildings would have done. And would not those major projects always be denied him, as for the most part they had been to Erith?

Erith was not unknown in the world of architecture. He was a Royal Academician and a member of the Royal Fine Art Commission. He built the Wolfson Building at Lady Margaret Hall, Oxford, and Jack Straw's Castle in Hampstead. He reconstructed Nos. 10, 11 and 12 Downing Street. But his absolute rejection of the Modern Movement in favour of Classicism cut him off from many of the opportunities available to mainstream architects. It was a fat time for architecture but very few of the chances went Erith's way. His practice was small. Sometimes work dried up altogether. Interest in Classicism seemed to decline rather than increase during the 1960s. Then his death coincided with the energy crisis of 1973, which frightened off many potential private clients. There was a real likelihood that Terry's practice would have been even more difficult than his predecessor's.

We now know that it did not turn out like that. With what might, and to Terry quite possibly does, seem the unexpectedness of divine providence, a commission to detail an immense temple in the Middle East gave succour for five years – a time when there was very little else to keep the office going. Then gradually it seemed that interest in Terry's kind of architecture was increasing in Britain. He found himself asked to design a number of significant country houses. In contrast to Erith, who was retiring by nature, he took off his coat and got down into the cockpit of office building in London. Now that public taste has changed in a way that would have been unforeseeable twenty years ago and it is possible to speak of a Classical Revival in British architecture, Terry is the leading figure of the movement. It would be wrong to say that this is a position he sought, as he would have continued in exactly the same manner architecturally whether there had been a revival or not. Indeed talk of personal success in the world embarrasses him, unless there is due acknowledgement of 'the One who gives success'. But since a revival of Classicism has, as it were, happened around him, work has increasingly flowed his way. His staff has expanded to fill all the available room in his office and has overflowed to an annexe to his house; they have been on overtime since 1984 – beginning at 8.30 am, finishing at 6.30 pm and working a half day on Saturdays; and Terry is designing a major office development in London, new buildings for a Cambridge college, several country houses including one in the United States, and a host of large and small Classical projects for the time being kept under wraps.

To write a book about an architect who is still, like Terry, under fifty may seem premature. Architects begin late: they have a long training and it is likely to take them several years to get into their stride once they have started work. But in this case the subject is quite simply – and apart from anything else he may be – a phenomenon. His approach to architecture has been worlds apart from that of most architects of his generation; so has the pattern of his career. Behind the buildings lie the strengths of his erudition in terms of Classical architecture and his intense religious belief. These repay analysis. And when the full range of buildings is looked at as a whole, one can see the workings of a distinct and individual architectural personality, strikingly different from either eighteenth- or early twentieth-century predecessors.

For Terry is no simple Classicist. It would be nearer the mark to call him a Mannerist, because of his preference on the one hand for simple plan forms and Palladian proportions, and on the other for the richest Classical detail culled from a very wide range of sources: some early and pure, some late and debased. It is as though he has a spiritual hunger for Classicism and devours Classical ideas in all shapes and forms. Whether he is in Florence, Venice, Essex or London, looking at a Renaissance church or a nineteenth-century gentleman's club, he always dis-covers something to feast upon. There is also the Picturesque aspect of his work. Despite the (to a modern age) rarefied learning of his detail, and his craftsman-like insistence on sound, traditional building, he still harbours a feeling for contrasts reminiscent of the great master showman Nash.

PREFACE

For the last two thousand years all Classical architecture has relied upon precedent; architects have looked back from one age to another and taken elements from the language of their predecessors to enrich their own. In the late twentieth century, however, some people have difficulty in accepting an architecture like Terry's that is based on a wide experience of the past, although wholly original in the way that experience is used. 'Never look back' we were urged by the sons of the Modern Movement, although they, of course, looked back to the buildings of Le Corbusier and their other heroes as much as a Classicist would look back to Rome. More recently post-Modernism has had a liberating effect: its adherents enjoy quoting from the past and do so with gusto. But their aim is only to evoke a general mood – like the violinist in a restaurant who brings back memories of holidays in Italy – rather than to understand and develop the principles of Classicism, which are an expression of the logic of traditional building. When Terry's work is discussed, one sooner or later hears the word 'pastiche', as though he were trying to make his buildings look as though they might have been built in, say, the eighteenth century. People who make that criticism only betray their own visual illiteracy. They know too little about the eighteenth century and other Classical periods to understand the extent to which Terry's architecture is different.

One should be wary of making historical comparisons too glibly. Some critics have an absurd habit of saying: 'Soane would not have done that,' or 'Wren would not have done this' – when they are probably completely ignorant of the conditions of the commission. The geniuses of Classical architecture have appeared very few times in a century, even when the Classical tradition was in full spate. But in some ways the towering figures of the past had an easier time of it than the lonely disciple of today. For they had the confidence of working in a world in which the values of Classicism were so much accepted as to be almost in the blood. They could draw on an army of masons and other craftsmen with a shared knowledge of Classical forms. Above all they had the opportunities to build. Different conditions have pertained over the past forty years. Terry has a distrust of the concept of genius, if it means prima donna-ish displays of wilfulness and temperament. His ideal is closer to that of the craftsman or masterbuilder. If the historical comparison has to be made – and perhaps to some degree it is inevitable, since there are few contemporary architects against whose work Terry's can be judged – we would do well to turn the pages of Howard Colvin's *Biographical Dictionary of English Architects*, with an eye on the numerous entries of two or three columns. These were the good but not outstanding Georgian architects; they

3

may perhaps be called the Georgian average. What is to be made of Terry when we set him beside this yardstick? It is extraordinary to think that, even with all the disadvantages that a contemporary Classicist suffers, Terry would already have notched up a page or two in Colvin's great work. His personality as a Classicist would also have called for more analysis than many the Georgian average warrants. Supporters of the Classical Revival in the twentieth century regret that Terry is not embedded in the security of a living tradition, with many other classical architects practising in other Classical manners with equal flair. We should be all the more grateful to him for his courage and perseverance. For the least that can be said of Terry's achievement is that his example has demonstrated that there is still an alternative to the ruinous architectural orthodoxies that have created so much ugliness and misery since the Second World War; he is one of the few who has kept hope alive, showing that Britain can still be beautiful.

Terry would be the first to admit that each job he undertakes is accorded greater attention than it would have been in previous ages because he is one of the few Classicists around. While an architect like Soane, for example is known to have worked on about a hundred country houses Terry has to date built less than ten. Consequently every one of Terry's works has been scrutinized in far greater detail than the everyday commissions of an eighteenth- or nineteenth-century architect would have been. One slip and the whole Classical Revival is condemned. A more legitimate criticism of modern Classical architecture – Terry's sometimes included – is that, since the opportunities are few, there is a tendency to cram too much architecture into too small a commission. Sometimes this is true of the country houses, which, though beautifully crafted and built of the best materials, can have a sense of being miniatures, because the ideas are too grand for the scale. This is surely a forgivable fault in an architect who is bursting to build. For any architect, the great thing about having more work on hand is that there is also more opportunity to learn by experience. One of the pleasures of studying Terry's work at a time when he is busier than ever before is that one can see the process of learning taking place. Merks Hall, one of his latest jobs, is a better house than Waverton, one of his first and most illustrated – fine though that is too in its way. His already highly developed personality as a Classicist is still developing in intriguing ways. It will be one of the pleasures of the remaining years of the twentieth century to see how it unfolds. And all the more so if his ambitions for the Classical Revival come to pass. Having scented success in the field of office development he is now straining at the leash to take on other challenges: a hospital, perhaps, or an airport. Even motorway flyovers could benefit from the

PREFACE

Classicist's improving hand.

To judge from the amount of comment his buildings excite and the frequency with which they are illustrated, even Terry's architectural opponents (and most certainly they do exist) must regard them as striking a particular chord with late-twentieth-century taste. For perhaps the most remarkable aspect of the whole story is the present popularity of Terry's work with the public – a fact reflected in the origin of this book. The idea came neither from Terry nor myself but from my editor, Stephen Davies of Viking Penguin. I take this as proof that Terry is no longer a minority taste of architectural enthusiasts but a figure of importance to the larger world.

For help with the preparation of this book I would like to thank, firstly, the owners of the houses who generously gave me permission to visit them. My thanks must also go to Christine Terry for having fed me on the numerous Saturdays which I disrupted with my tape-recorder. I am grateful to Lucy Archer for having allowed me to read the manuscript of her architectural biography of her father, *Raymond Erith, Architect*, before publication. This is of course the canonical account of Erith's *œuvre*, and, knowing it would appear, I decided to limit my book to Quinlan Terry's own work – although no description of Terry could ignore Erith as his all-important mentor. Having once been asked to write the book for Viking, I have been encouraged along the way by Alan Powers, with whom I have discussed many points and who read the manuscript. My wife Naomi must also be thanked for her patience during my absences both in Dedham and at the word-processor.

CLIVE ASLET

1. *Fantasy of the House of Joy, 1958*

CHAPTER ONE

BEGINNINGS

Some of John Quinlan Terry's earliest memories are of being snowed up with his parents on a hillside near Whipsnade Zoo, where they had been evacuated from London during the Second World War. They were staying in the house built by Berthold Lubetkin for himself. With the Terrys were the Modernist architect Ernö Goldfinger and his family. The recollections are not what you would expect in someone who is pre-eminent, in some quarters even notorious, as a Classicist and a champion of tradition. For the Whipsnade 'Dacha', with its flat roof and white reinforced-concrete walls, was among the most aggressively avant-garde buildings of the mid-1930s. 'The designer admits that he has not capitulated to the accidents of a site which was forced on him,' wrote the Russian émigré in notes on his much-publicized dwelling; 'he excavated 800 yards of dazzling white chalk full of megalithic fossils to make a flat lawn and a flat house – where any Czech would have made a house in steps topped by a roof garden.'

By contrast the house where Terry, born in 1937, grew up was more sympathetic to his later thinking. It stood in an ordinary London stock-brick terrace of about 1810. There were two rooms to each main floor and a passage with the staircase at the side. It was undistinguished, but pleasing, sensible and economical, and it showed how a simple form of Classicism could lend dignity to a relatively modest house, even where a degree of asymmetry was determined by the plan. Terry's bedroom was on the second floor with that of his sister; his parents had the front room on the first floor, with its sash-windows down to the floor and little cast-iron balconies. 'That house was about as well designed and sensibly constructed as any I have known,' Terry has written. 'It had that comforting feeling of commonsense and moderation based on experience which no architect nowadays could ever attain; particularly because it was free from that conceit and self-consciousness which influenced building from about 1837 onwards.' At the back there was a little garden, at the front an area and an even smaller garden between that and the street. The young Terry used to watch red admirals and peacock butterflies on the large buddleia by the gate.

What spanned the gulf between this house and that at Whipsnade? The brick house was in Downshire Hill in Hampstead, and Terry's parents shared many of the values of the Hampstead intelligentsia between the wars. Terry's father was a solicitor, his mother a talented artist. They read the *Signature*. They knew Gropius, whom they met in the United States, and were closely involved with Jack Pritchard, the entrepreneur behind Wells Coates's Lawn Road flats and the Isokon furniture firm. They belonged to the English Folk Dance and Song Society; they visited Russia. If not formally atheist, they were sufficiently opposed to organized religion not to have a church wedding or to have their children christened. When it came to choosing a public school for their son they decided on Bryanston – not quite as progressive as Bedales, where his father had gone, but in similar mould.

So Terry was not brought up as a natural traditionalist from all points of view. The force of character and independence of mind that allowed him to become one were encouraged by a childhood illness that cast a shadow over his first years at Bryanston. For two years he was deaf. Although he fully recovered, isolation in a world without sound, followed by the effort of will necessary to recover his hearing, left him with the inner toughness required by a Classicist in the late 1960s, before hope of a Classical Revival had dawned. Otherwise, Terry's principal memory of Bryanston is of the sculptorium, where every minute that could be snatched from lessons or games he spent stone-carving – at one point even worrying his father that he might become a sculptor. The sculpture master, Don Potter,

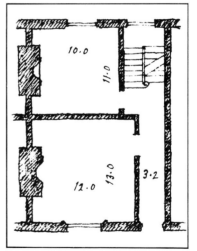

2. The house in Downshire Hill

a pupil of Eric Gill, was an early influence; he taught him that application and self-discipline were, in the arts, sometimes rarer qualities than genius. But from the earliest days, at least from the age of four, Terry had always known he would become an architect.

Leaving school he went in 1955 to the Architectural Association. This was dominated by the spirit of the Bauhaus, which must already have been familiar from Downshire Hill. By the end of his first three years Terry had discovered his own direction sufficiently to know that the teachings of Modernism had little to offer him.

Two friendships, with Andrew Anderson and Malcolm Higgs, encouraged him along this path. Together the three students formed a group known to themselves, in an architectural pun, as the Force Triangle. For a time they had been called the Flowerpot, following a first-year collage project; to others they were simply the Christian Weirdies. They tended to wear stiff collars and identical red neckties bought, though you would not have thought it, from army surplus. Anderson was the leader. Like Terry he made linocuts – a technique which, when Terry went to join Raymond Erith in Dedham, would bear fruit in Erith and Terry's annual Classical contribution to the Royal Academy's architectural room. At the AA however, the emphasis of the Force Triangle was on Arts and Crafts. They admired William Morris, then moved on to Eric Gill. They were excited by Lutyens and stayed in Lindisfarne Castle. Sometimes Terry and Anderson would 'become' the figures they idealized. Terry might play Philip Webb to Anderson's Morris, for example: roles which typified their relationship. In friendship, religion and work, Terry has a willingness to submit to authority. The group combined on measured drawings, including Seaton Delaval Hall – but with no serious conversations about Classicism. Friends say that at this time Terry even admired flats by Connell, Ward and Lucas in Ferdinand Street near the Round House.

The preferences of the Force Triangle were austere. They were less interested in joining gentlemen's clubs or drinking claret (activities one might associate with traditionalism) than in walking under the moonlight across Dartmoor, bicycling to the docks or living rough – they slept in haystacks even in winter. They were not without a sense of humour and a particular sense of style, but there was also a passionately earnest streak. Terry, somewhat to his parents' concern, was developing the extreme religious convictions that were to become the unshakeable guiding principles of his life. Andrew Anderson had introduced him to the Westminster Chapel where the famous Welsh evangelical preacher Dr Martyn Lloyd-Jones held congregations spellbound. Terry also attended seminars held by Dr Lloyd-Jones's son-in-law (Sir) Fred Catherwood. Here the message was of a God of order – the Supreme Designer; His character showed itself in the harmony and repose of Nature, although the modern world, and perhaps modern tendencies in art and architecture, seemed given over to irrationality and anxiety. In a self-consistent theology, argued Catherwood, religion must be the factor that

3. Wallpaper, 1964 (linocut)

brings all aspects of life into accord. In the course of time Terry was to discover how his theology could interpenetrate his work as well as his life, and to evolve a theory of Classicism that made the orders appear not only uniquely compatible with the intentions of the Creator but possibly even divinely inspired (as shall be described in Chapter 11). However, for the time being Classicism lay still in the future, when the authority would be that of the anti-clerical Erith.

Another important influence, and one that perhaps also tended to his eventual Classicism, arrived in Terry's second year at the AA, in the shape of a young and even younger-looking Polish girl, Christine Marie-Thérèse de Ruttié, who was descended from one of Napoleon's generals. Terry was to marry her in 1961. Christine had already studied architecture at the Warsaw Academy where, in complete contrast to the architectural schools of Western Europe, the principles of the Beaux-Arts still held good. Warsaw, it should be remembered, did not suffer the misguided redevelopment of London after the war, but was with loving piety repaired street by street, building by building. To practise Classicism in the second

10

half of the twentieth century seemed far less surprising to her than it would have done to someone brought up in England.

Terry did not find his fourth and fifth years at the AA stimulating. He was taught successively by John Killick, of Howell, Killick and Partridge, and Peter Smithson – two of the leading exponents of the New Brutalist style – but, in common with his contemporaries, he spent no more than a couple of days a week in Bedford Square: the rest of his time was spent in the office of James Stirling and James Gowan. They were then designing the disastrous Leicester Engineering Laboratories, which won every architectural prize at the time. Terry also had a year out in an office in Oxford in 1958–9. There he made measured drawings of Butterfield's Keble College – his liking for which must have seemed highly radical. His sense of hopelessness at the state of architecture was expressed in a linocut called 'The House of Joy'. In it a Nonconformist chapel which Terry had measured in Oxford – a simple brick building with a pediment, symbolizing the right values of the world and spirit – is seen in a state of desolation, with brambles climbing over the front. Everywhere are Biblical texts from the minor prophets describing ruin and decay. The House waits for regeneration: 'Until the Spirit be poured upon us from on high & the wilderness be a fruitful field & the fruitful field be counted for a forest.' It seemed that it would wait in vain. For his finals at the AA Terry prepared a scheme in a Philip Webb-inspired style, curiously similar to the neo-Vernacular of recent years, which was failed as being historicist. Realizing that it was essential to obtain a qualification he submitted to the yoke and got out a Modernist scheme, which was passed. His tutors thought he had seen the light.

After the AA Terry spent a year in C. H. Elsom's office, where the work was mainly large-scale office development. He spent several weeks measuring the square footage of the buildings then occupying the site of the present Army and Navy stores, in the effort to convince the ground landlords that the return from redevelopment would be higher than from retaining the existing structures. This at least taught him how the office developer's mind works and how his money is made. The experience gained at Elsom's has now at last been put to use in Dufours Place and the £19 million Richmond Riverside development. But it is not surprising that Terry found this period acutely depressing and even considered leaving architecture altogether, as he found that 'you end up building the things you hate'. Terry's unhappiness became known to the architect John Brandon-Jones, who continued the practice originally founded by C. F. A. Voysey. Christine had entered his office and in the months before their marriage the couple frequently baby-sat for the Brandon-Jones children. It was Brandon-Jones who suggested that Terry should meet Raymond Erith. 'Terry spent a year ... in Oxford and more recently he has been with Elsom in London where he has had experience of a rather different sort of building,' wrote Brandon-Jones in a letter of introduction of 23 June 1962. 'He told me the other day that he was feeling more and more strongly that his real interest was in designing buildings to be built by craftsmen rather than in producing plans for the assembly of ready made details, and that his ultimate aim was to run a personal practice, if possible outside London.'

The Terrys and all the Brandon-Jones children accordingly set off for Dedham in Terry's 1929 open Alvis Speed 20, and because of problems with the car arrived uncharacteristically late. Christine and the children spent the day on the river: Terry lunched with Erith, who was enjoying his role as paterfamilias at the head of a table of twelve. After lunch Erith and Terry walked down to Erith's farm, lay down in a field and talked about architecture. It was decided that Terry should move to Dedham and join him. The introduction had been a generous act on Brandon-Jones's part. Christine naturally went with her husband to Essex, and Brandon-Jones had one less assistant.

4. 'Long Live Laura', 1964 (linocut)

CHAPTER TWO

RAYMOND ERITH
AND THE MOVE TO DEDHAM

Terry's first experience of Erith's buildings had come at the AA. A sympathetic tutor told him that, if he was really intent on traditionalism, he might do well to go and see some of Erith's 'housing' (these were the socially conscious 1950s) in Aubrey Walk on Campden Hill. Terry, Higgs and Anderson dutifully went off on their bicycles and, Terry has recalled, 'saw a terrace of three houses in London stock brick, Flemish bond, sash windows and slate roof: built, we thought, about 1790? – and on the other side of the road a new block of flats complete with concrete balconies, picture windows and flat roofs. I can well remember the three of us standing with our backs to Raymond's building and discussing our surprise and disappointment at what we thought was his work!' That response was really a fine compliment to Erith, for the Aubrey Walk houses epitomize the scholarly sensitivity and discrimination for which he was praised even by Modernists.

Erith's story has been told in the recent biography by his daughter, Lucy Archer. He was born in 1904 and had little formal schooling owing to ill health from tuberculosis, which left him permanently crippled in his left arm and lame in his left leg. After the AA he worked for Morley Horder (who, as Mrs Archer writes, had the habit of posting Erith's salary cheques down a crack at the back of the fireplace, until finally the mantelpiece was removed to reclaim them). His ambition was probably to design great public buildings and he entered a number of competitions for work of this kind. But circumstances decreed otherwise. His first important work on his own, two lodges for Windsor Great Park, set the tone for his later practice, which was almost entirely devoted to country houses and estate work. As a royal commission, the lodges should also have established his reputation; but it was typical of Erith that, though the King and his household were not known for a deep understanding of architecture, he chose to design them in his austerest Soanic style. This was appropriate because, by eighteenth-century standards, they were simply un-grand rural buildings, of an almost utilitarian nature. But events showed that untutored twentieth-century expectations were different. By an appalling stroke of bad luck the lodges were bombed in 1940 only a fortnight after completion, removing the best advertisement an architect of Erith's stamp could have hoped for. When they were reconstructed after the Second World War, Sidney Tatchell and Son were employed: their more obviously winning neo-Regency mode was clearly better adapted to royal taste.

The early and middle 1950s were an extremely lean time for Erith. Having bought a farm before the war, he considered giving up architecture altogether and devoting himself to rearing a pedigree herd. Towards the end of the decade work began to pick up, and a highly prestigious job came in the commission to reconstruct the most famous of all Georgian town houses in Britain: Nos. 10, 11 and 12 Downing Street. These were still going through the office when Terry arrived: Terry detailed the kitchen fittings.

But even after Downing Street work was not plentiful. Much of the load of the office was absurdly mundane – 'dozens of odd jobs, bathrooms, smoking chimneys, leaky roofs and the rest'. Both before and after Terry arrived Erith worked on numerous projects that were never carried out. It was intensely frustrating, for Erith above all wanted to build. Sometimes he would be almost reduced to tears. But as a result he had time on his hands: time that he could spend endlessly revising his designs, always paring them away to get at the architectural essence, and in writing letters to clients explaining minutely why some particular detail – a bookcase, a gatepier – had come out as it had, for there was a reason behind everything.

At Dedham, Terry quickly came to share Erith's passion for Classicism; working closely with him in an office remote from other influences, and by nature inclined to an attitude of submission towards authorities that he respected (in religion, friendship and architecture), he also came to absorb other aspects of the Erith persona such as his drawing style – and perhaps even his handwriting and liking for tweeds. Erith quickly saw in Terry a possible partner who would continue the practice, and he treated him with fatherly kindness. Terry was prepared to sit at Erith's feet. The relationship was close. Terry cannot remember a single occasion on which they quarrelled. Yet temperamentally the two men were far less similar than is sometimes assumed. Erith had an instinct for the good things of life: he kept a cellar, loved travel, drove a vintage Bentley (in Italy people would break into spontaneous applause as he passed) and his attitude to God – or the gods – was pantheistic. He had a sceptical view of the clergy. By contrast Terry, it seemed

5. Croquet shed at Aynho, 1966 (linocut)

15

to Erith, was almost fanatical in his religion and scarcely less austere in his way of life. Then when it came to architecture their preferences were reversed. It was Erith who eschewed ornament, Terry who had the feeling for the Baroque.

Erith had been young in the 1920s and 1930s. Although he had rejected Modernism, he had agonized over it. To some extent this coloured his Classicism. His early buildings showed great admiration for the work of Soane. Erith saw Soane as the last point before the Classical tradition began to decay. This gave his late-Georgian-inspired work a more rigorous, intellectual caste than that of the Regency Revival – or what Osbert Lancaster called 'Vogue Regency' – of fashionable inter-war architects such as Oliver Hill and Gerald Wellesley and Trenwith Wells. As he grew older he found that his taste was increasingly drawn further back in time and further south in geography, towards the inspiration of so much English Classicism – Palladio. The Palladio he wished to revive was the Palladio of the simple country villas of the Veneto, not the Palladianism of marmoreal English country houses: 'Even Palladio's grandest villas were always houses of the country: farm houses really, with a farmyard in front and colonnades which were really cart lodges and Dutch barns.' He had a special feeling for genuinely rural architecture, being himself a farmer, and the simplicity also appealed.

Erith would continually go back over his work, generally to remove decoration. The Pediment, Aynho, a few hundred yards from Aynho Park which Soane remodelled, is best known from the witty croquet pavilion, but the house itself was one of Erith's driest works – although greatly enjoyed by the clients. Terry, who has in recent years been busier than Erith ever was, has been inclined to react against this tendency. 'To revise a design once or twice can improve it,' he says, 'but to go back six or seven times may kill the first spark.'

Erith also had a streak of rationalism which he inherited, ultimately, from the Gothic Revival. On occasion he would offend the Georgian Group and other sticklers for symmetry by designing elevations that almost wilfully did not balance. Wivenhoe New Park, where an arcaded garage is not mirrored in the guest flat on the other side of the main block, is an example. Terry, again, is ruled more by visual than intellectual considerations. In his Frog Meadow houses, the Baha'i temple and the Nash-like Richmond Riverside development his use of incident has been more wholeheartedly Picturesque in spirit than Erith would have countenanced. Erith's visual escape valve, so to speak, came in the wit of 'instant history'. The Aynho croquet pavilion was built in the form of a big, mid-Georgian rusticated gatepier around which had been erected a Victorian shed with a Cotswold stone roof, with a still later iron bench around that. At Shottesbrooke in

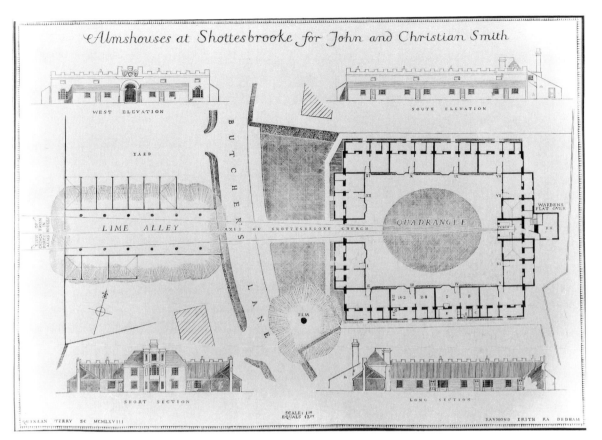

6. Design for (unbuilt) almshouses at Shottesbrooke, 1968

Berkshire, in a group of almshouses designed for John Smith of the Landmark Trust, Erith turned the Modernist cry which he seemed to hear everywhere, that you had to be outward-looking and forward-looking, on its head: the almshouses, he declared, would be inward-looking and backward-looking. They were to have been built round a square courtyard the wall of which, it was imagined, could have belonged to a Roman vineyard; at some point settlers had come and made a dwelling within this wall, with lean-to sheds on the outside (in fact containing bathrooms and kitchens) and a crenellated parapet, supposedly eighteenth-century, on top. But in 1968 the county planning authorities were not ready for the inward and backward look, and the design was refused planning permission – even though the client was building on his own land and at his own expense.

Erith took an amused attitude towards his young apprentice's greater taste for flamboyance in Classicism. When Erith had been young, Modernism had been fresh and challenging; but by the time Terry had got to the AA, it had become an

17

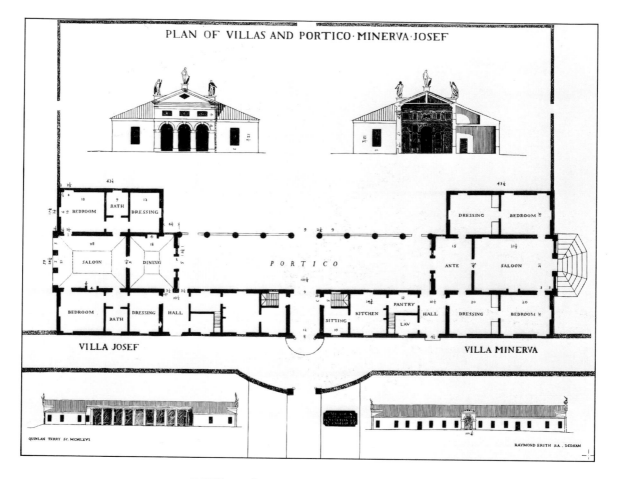

7. Villa and Portico Minerva and Josef, 1966

entrenched monopoly. Terry rejected not just its forms but its deepest principles. Rebellion led to the Baroque. Erith would tease him by saying he was a Jesuit. 'Isn't this a good example of *le style* Terry?' wrote Erith on a postcard of the fabulously rich Hôtel de Ville at La Rochelle – adding: 'Actually I am not sure that it is not *moderne*, great expanses of glass.' When passing a particularly elaborate building Erith would remark: 'There but for the grace of me go you.' But, equally, when Erith perceived a direction in Terry's taste which he did not think dangerous he would encourage it, even if it did not agree with his own. Thus, as a consequence of his liking for Gothic, he took pains to introduce Gothic, or at least Gothick, details into the designs so that Terry had a chance to research them. At Knight's Hill near Buntingford, in Hertfordshire, the country house with which John Profumo and his wife Valerie Hobson occupied themselves after the former's retirement from public life, Tudor-style window openings were

18

introduced (though typically these were given sashes, as though the Tudor work had been altered in the seventeenth century, and there was a top storey with *œil-de-bœufs* to suggest that an owner in the eighteenth century had had a big family). This led Terry to draw the windows at Hadleigh Deanery nearby, and subsequently to spend long, rewarding hours detailing the shaped and moulded bricks for the surrounds. At one point when there was little other work they spent a week driving around the churches of Essex to detail a niche for Dedham church: the old niche had been completely worn away and the stonemason who had been asked to replace it had no grasp of Gothic. An exercise like this showed that, even in little things, there was usually more to old work than at first met the eye.

Cribs always played an essential part in Erith's designing, and his way of work has been inherited by Terry. Having established the plan and section he would begin on the elevation, which reflected the other two. At this point he would consult sourcebooks and his own sketchbooks to see how the great architects and, with all their practical knowledge, the mastermasons of the past had tackled the problems of design that he was facing. The premise was always that the novel idea, being untried, was likely to work less well than something that had been approved by use and time. This was the strength of working in a tradition: you had access to the accumulated wisdom of two thousand years and did not need to go through the risky, trial-and-error process of attempting to invent new ways and forms for yourself. The obvious truth of this is seen in constructional techniques – how to detail a sash-window, how to build a wall (see Chapter 10). To architects for whom Classicism is a living language, which they are nevertheless concerned to speak correctly and sanely, the same applies to the use of Classical detail. Among the printed books most often referred to were Palladio's *Quattro Libri*, the 1825 Paris edition of *Palladio's Works*, the 1832 Venice edition of *Sanmicheli's Works*, *Letarouilly's Five Books*, as well as more standard works on the Orders and measured drawings of Roman architecture.[1]

When Terry came to the office his AA training had left him with the knowledge that there were three Classical orders, but not five. Knowledge and skill were acquired through a working relationship like that of master and apprentice in the eighteenth century. Until Erith's death in 1973 – even after Terry had become a partner in 1966 – the grand lines of the design were always established by Erith. Terry worked on drawing up details, at first only realizing Erith's vision, then, as he grew in ability and in understanding of Erith's mind, bringing his own

---

1. Terry has described the Erith office in the introduction to the 1976 Royal Academy exhibition 'Raymond Erith RA (1904–1973)'.

experience to bear. The drawings always had to pass the test of an Erith critique; but after a number of years this was more likely to take the shape of a discussion between two seekers after the truth, rather than the handing down of truth from the older to the younger man. Erith's skill as a draughtsman was superb, but this began to be equalled by Terry, who was also, it came to be admitted, better at lettering. In due course the two men thought along such similar lines that they could work together on the same drawing – one finishing the other's work. Terry usually did the lettering, with the result that it is now sometimes extremely difficult, even for the surviving partner, to tell who did what.

In comparison to most modern offices, Erith's might seem authoritarian; but he was quick to accept that Terry could bring something of his own. The linocuts are an example of this. Erith rapidly saw that the technique could give a rendering of a building somewhat similar to that in Palladio's *Quattro Libri*; the strikingly intense black and intense white (Terry used machine glazed paper to enhance this effect) would focus attention on the essence of architecture – solid and void. So from the year after Terry joined the office the linocut was the medium employed for the office's Royal Academy submission. However, Erith demanded a far greater refinement of line than Terry's more Arts and Crafts work had been given hitherto.

Erith was generous in the help he gave to his protégé. For their home, the Terrys had found a lovely, rambling sixteenth-century farmhouse on the edge of Dedham with the poetic name of Winterfloods; but it was in a primitive state of repair and had – worse – been given a brick front in 1906. Here in the early 1960s – a few years before the Back to the Earth trend had turned into a cliché – they grew their own vegetables, baked their own bread and rejected the synthetic materials of the modern world. When Erith examined the building, he declared that what it needed was a decent door in the middle and sash-windows. Once more Terry found that his time at the AA had left him wholly unequipped to tackle these apparently simple vernacular problems. Every Saturday morning, therefore, Erith would work with Terry on the details for Winterfloods, with Erith drawing most of them; so that Terry's work there became an object lesson in practical building. (Even after the restoration, however, the mood of Winterfloods was 'scrubbed boards and poverty', with rush mats over brick floors. The extremism charmed Erith, though again it was not his own approach.)

It was not of course Erith's fault that his knowledge sometimes seemed overwhelming. In the early years Terry could not help feeling at times slightly depressed to observe that, while Erith seemed to have all the answers to the problems of Classicism, he himself could find none. Little by little, as his experience and confidence increased, that apprehension was allayed. He found that, gradually, he was able to approach questions like the choice of the most appropriate Ionic order, or the correct spacing of windows in a room, in the spirit of his master. A turning point as far as his own confidence went was the experience of four months at the fountainhead – measuring ancient and Renaissance buildings in Rome.

8. St John's, Downshire Hill, 1961

9. Santa Maria del Popolo:
detail of door by Bernini, 1983

10. Arch with pierced
surround by Bramante, 1967

CHAPTER THREE

THE ROMAN SKETCHBOOK

Shortly before Raymond Erith died he had a dream. He dreamt that he was in a massive conclave of architects. They were all there – Lasdun, Spence, Casson, every celebrity of the profession who was alive at the time. And a great figure from the past, as it might be Vitruvius, came down to speak. He went up to Erith and said that, really, he was not much good, he had got this, this and this wrong in his work, and he had not spent enough time measuring Classical buildings – particularly drawing them in a sketchbook on the spot, to scale. This was the message Erith felt he had to deliver the next day to Quinlan Terry: measure, measure, measure Classical buildings, and always draw them to scale. Not, however, that it had been a wholly depressing dream. Erith said that he had woken up feeling elated. For while the Vitruvius figure had told Erith that his architecture was less than perfect, he had not spoken to the other architects present at all.

The Vitruvian exhortation of Erith's dream may have reinforced Terry in his conviction that the measuring of ancient and Renaissance buildings was to be one of the keys to his development. In order to become part of the Classical tradition, he had first to acquire an intimate knowledge of what previous generations had done. He felt he had to rediscover for himself the principles of Classicism in what seemed their purest form. From the Renaissance onwards succeeding generations of Classicists had sought to do this by studying the work of the ancients. They had also acquired a vocabulary of details – cornices, door frames, balusters, urns – by cribbing the best examples of past work. To a twentieth-century architect the range of possible precedents was extended almost limitlessly by the Classicism of the Renaissance itself, not to mention that of the sixteenth to nineteenth centuries. Only by instilling in himself a detailed knowledge of what was, so to speak, on offer could Terry decide what to build on, what to reject and what to borrow. It is true that since the days of Palladio quantities of Classical buildings had been measured and the results often beautifully engraved, so that in many cases Terry could have used data that was already extant. But, apart from naturally wanting the enjoyment of direct contact with the buildings themselves, he was reluctant to trust material gathered by others. When an opportunity to measure buildings in Rome on a scholarship came in 1967, he found that his scepticism was proved right.

Quinlan and Christine arrived in Rome in October and stayed until the following February. These months of intensive study of Roman buildings had a considerable influence on Terry's architectural character. In one way in particular this was later to become independent of Erith's. While Erith, as we have seen, first sought to go back to Soane as the last Classicist in the great tradition then looked increasingly to what he saw as the essentially country architecture of Palladio, Terry has not been afraid on occasion to draw on the more full-blooded traditions. Taken as a whole his work has a more consistently Italianate flavour than that of Erith, with his special feeling for the local architecture of Suffolk.

On his return Terry assembled the information he had collected in an unpublished album called the 'Roman Sketchbook'. Looking through it today, one is struck by the variety of buildings he thought it worth his while to measure. Terry has the reputation of being not just a Classicist, but a Classicist in the most austere of moulds. But even in 1967 he was looking at Hellenistic and eighteenth-century Baroque buildings, as well as Imperial and early Renaissance works. Beyond a ravenous curiosity about Classicism of all kinds, two external factors encouraged this breadth of taste. For one thing the Terrys' flat was in Trastevere, which happens to be a largely eighteenth-century district. So it was natural for Terry to study a church like Sant'Agata in Trastevere, which he walked past every day. He found that in the end its restlessness palled, but the memory of the mouldings has stayed with him. A detail similar to the guttae in the capitals of the doorcase – a distortion of the Classical language derived from Michelangelo – is used in the Richmond Riverside development. This building also helped teach him, incidentally, that bold plain mouldings should be used on a long building, which would otherwise become over-linear, and that thin ones are acceptable only on a building with many breaks backwards and forwards.

The other influence towards diversity was quite simply the problem of access. What no book of measured drawings can show is perhaps the most time-consuming aspect of the work: the long afternoons spent in the corridors of the Comune di Roma waiting for a *permesso* to climb scaffolding or visit a site. Once official help was granted, it could be bounteous. Only with the assistance of the

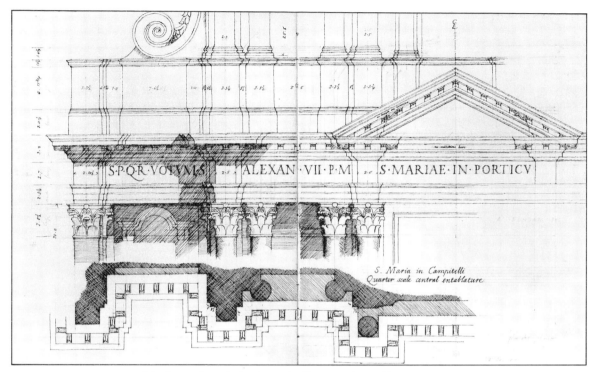

11. Santa Maria in Campitelli: central entablature, 1967

Rome fire brigade was it possible for Terry to ascend the Arch of Janus, for instance. But extending ladders and turntables were not always available and when Terry saw a monument already under scaffolding (there were fewer then in Italy than now) he liked to take advantage of the fact. That is why he measured the Jesuitical façade of Carlo Rainaldi's Santa Maria in Campitelli of about 1666. Also, in the periods between *permessi* Terry sometimes occupied himself by measuring a building as unastounding as the Belgian College in the Via del Quirinale – and even here the rustication would be turned to good account for Gray's Inn.

The obstacles to measuring were not only bureaucratic. The blistering cold of the Roman winter was another disincentive, although, typically, Terry faced its rigours with determination. Dressed in what friends referred to as a five-piece suit (coat and cap supplementing the usual three), he risked his life in clambering over the pantiled roof of the Pantheon when it was covered in ice. To have done anything less would have betrayed the example of Palladio, Sangallo and Peruzzi, who had also measured the cornice, if possibly under more clement conditions. On the other hand, scaffolding proved a benefit that predecessors could not have enjoyed. Sometimes it enabled him to make measurements that previous architects

25

could not have obtained. While Terry's measurements of the base of the Baptistery of Constantine agree with Palladio's, Palladio apparently sketched the building from the ground and therefore gave the order a Renaissance Composite capital. Terry – who was able to measure the building from a scaffolding erected, he was horrified to find out, to insert brown plate glass between the porphyry columns – discovered that it was much more Hellenistic, with, for instance, three rows of acanthus leaves rather than two (Figure 15).

On a number of occasions Terry was able to improve on the classic published information on Roman and Renaissance buildings because he was concerned solely with measuring architecture and made many of his drawings to scale on the spot, rather than with making a handsome engraved plate, perhaps in a different town and from measurements taken months before. His most satisfying discovery was of the subtleties that Bramante (one of Terry's particular heroes) introduced into the Chiocciola staircase in the Vatican (Figures 13–14). The staircase is a spiral lined with columns in a sequence of the orders; there are eight Tuscan, then eight Doric, eight Ionic and finally twelve Composite at the top. It was magnificently measured and engraved by Letarouilly, so it might have seemed unnecessary to measure it again. But Letarouilly shows all the columns of each order as being the same width; obviously he had only measured one and assumed that the others would be simple repeats. Bramante, however, was more sophisticated than that. If the widths had all been the same, there would have been a visual jolt as one order succeeded another. So the widths diminish fractionally as you move up the staircase. There are not five sizes of column but thirty-six. And that is not all. Because they are against a spiralling wall, the bases and caps of the columns are slightly wedge-shaped on plan, with the result that, in the Ionic and Composite orders, the volutes are slightly bigger at the front (towards the stair)

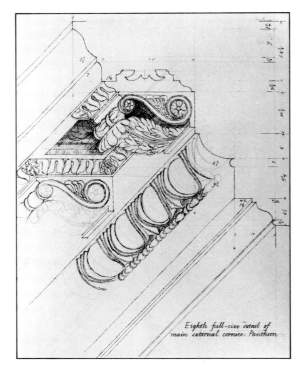

Eighth full-size detail of main external cornice. Pantheon

12. Pantheon: cornice

than at the back (towards the stairwell). 'One cannot help taking one's hat off to the architect,' wrote Terry in the Roman Sketchbook, 'such a simple looking design and yet achieved with the utmost care and thought, coupled with a masterly knowledge of construction.'

Terry has not so far had occasion to build a grand spiral staircase like the Chiocciola. But looking through the sketchbook almost twenty years on it is fascinating to see how many details have later cropped up in his work. On the way out to Rome he had stopped at Paris and got his hand in by measuring one of the seats in the Tuileries Gardens. When he returned to England, Erith used it in a garden in Walsham-le-Willows. Balusters from the Palazzo Vidoni were the crib for ones at Kings Walden Bury. The way in which, in the Nymphaeum at Genazzano (visited in a group led by Anthony Blunt), Bramante could make a cornice flow continuously into an impost has recurred several times – for instance in some of the doors at Waverton. A grotto fountain in the Via Garibaldi was Terry's introduction to false perspective and ultimately the inspiration for the Nymphaeum at West Green. Even though after a week spent measuring Fuga's Palazzo Corsini he was forced to conclude it was 'not a winner' (the perverse determination to be different for the sake of being different showed that 'the architect was obsessed with modernism'), nevertheless some of the plain, rather flat surrounds to windows and niches have been of use, again at Waverton, for example. Bramante's thick entablature, seen for instance at Santa Maria della Pace, has recently been used at Bengal House. Other ideas – like the rich effect of Rainaldi's pediment within a pediment – are being stored at the back of Terry's mind, awaiting only a suitable opportunity to pull them out onto the drawing board. ('When I see this I feel very deprived,' you are liable to hear Terry saying as he looks through an architectural book. ' I have not had a chance to do it yet.')

The Postscript to the Roman Sketchbook was developed into something of a manifesto of Terry's principles, which are those that have guided his subsequent career. The fact that Palladio gave the buildings of ancient Rome something of his own personality; that a Frenchman of the seventeenth century made the same monuments look authoritarian and academic; that, for all their accuracy, the nineteenth-century Englishmen Taylor and Cressy still made their drawings seem as though they might have been made of cast-iron: this showed that Classical architecture was 'a principle which is subject to changes in style ... While classical architecture is a principle its style evolves; its strength is that it can adapt itself to change without sacrificing its principle.' On all counts Classical architecture won out over Modernism. It employed building methods that would prove durable. It

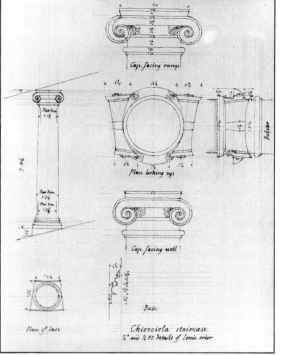

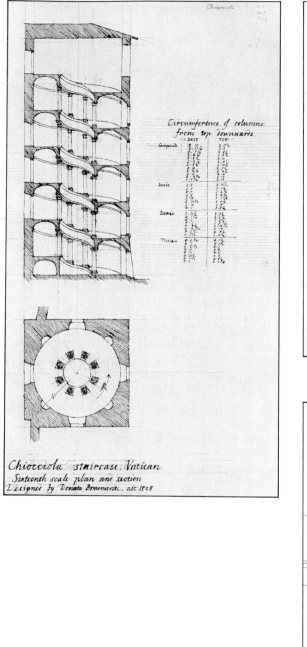

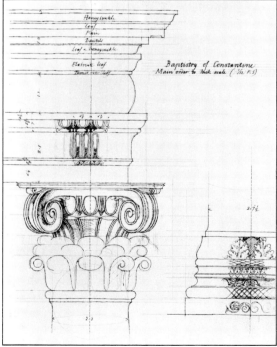

Chiocciola staircase, Vatican:
13. Section and plan (above)
14. Details of Ionic order (above right)

15. Baptistery of Constantine: main order (right)

was orderly whereas Modernism was chaotic. It had the flexibility to express different moods and purposes. It was based on nature. It was beautiful. The postscript ends by quoting Ecclesiastes 1.9–10. 'The thing that hath been, it is that which shall be; and that which is done is that which shall be done: and there is no new thing under the sun. Is there anything whereof it may be said, see, this is new? It hath been already of old time which was before us.' But what may seem most remarkable in the 1980s is that even in 1967 – when the architectural world was feasting itself on the South Bank arts centre, Cumbernauld New Town and the History Faculty building in Cambridge – the first glimmerings of a Classical revival could be detected. 'People are at last beginning to vent their dissatisfaction with the whole modern approach and to regard established modern architecture as inadequate,' he wrote. But one feels that by 'people', in this context, Terry can only have meant himself and a handful of friends.

16. San Eligio: seventeenth-century cupboard.

The real prospects for a Classical architect as they appeared at that date are shown in the letters Erith wrote Terry in the months before he returned home. Erith was particularly vulnerable to depression because of his own continuing illness, and there was talk of an operation. But even making allowance for that, the world as viewed from the office in Dedham seemed bleaker than ever. The collapse of the John Smith project at Shottesbrooke was a heavy blow. Erith was prone to worry – needlessly as it turned out – about the office finances. 'I have in fact felt at times there will be no practice left by the time you come back,' he wrote on 19 January 1968. In the same letter he urged Terry to change all his money into *lire*. 'I do not trust the £1 for a week: I mean it. The economy here is running down

Palazzo Corsini by Ferdinando Fuga.   1/500 scale

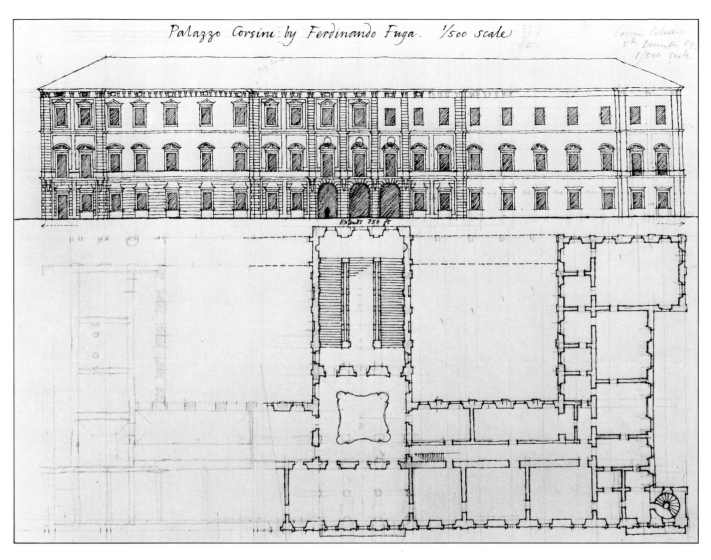

Extent 350 ft

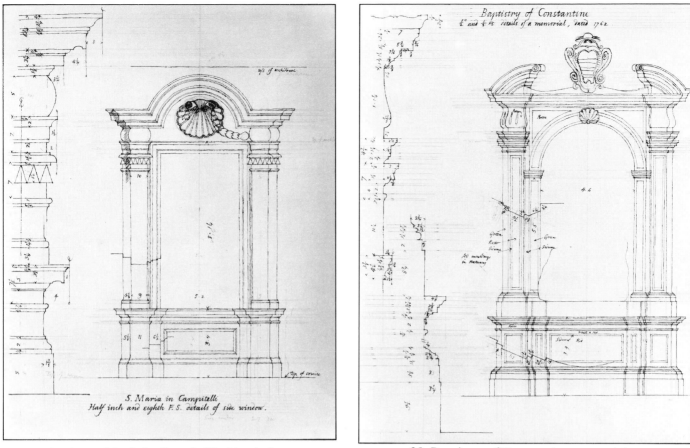

20. *Santa Maria in Campitelli: side window*

21. *Baptistery of Constantine: memorial*

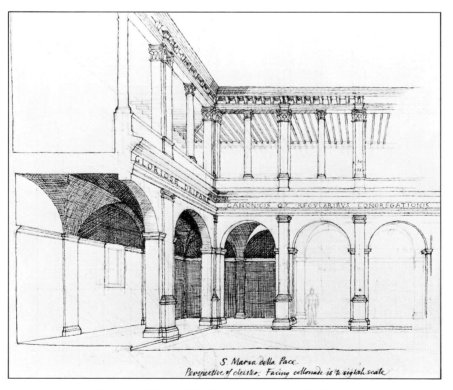

22. *Santa Maria della Pace: perspective of cloister*

FACING   *17. (above) Palazzo Corsini: plan and elevation, 1967*
18. (below left) Palazzo Corsini: niche on stairs, 1967. 19. (below right) Fountain in the Via Garibaldi, 1967

fast. There is no private building, or very little. The Govt. & their Housing Societies do it all. No good for Eriths.' The builders for one job sent 'dirty unhealthy boys with dirty girls hair ... Bring a pistol back with you please.'

A week later Erith was writing that it might be better if the whole political system of these, the Wilson years, was to collapse. After the Shottesbrooke fiasco he urged Terry to take up arms against 'the conviction that we *must*, absolutely and inevitably, have modern architecture ... the conviction that, however bad and unsatisfactory it may be, there *is no alternative*'. The tone seems almost hopeless.

And yet, and yet – hope was not given up altogether. '*Do* measure or draw cornices like this [he sketched an outline] with or without the complete entablature. They will be useful,' he wrote in the same letter. 'Also do try to see how the roof fits over the rooms.'

CHAPTER FOUR

KINGS WALDEN BURY

There was one ray of hope in the office. While Terry was in Rome, Sir Thomas Pilkington, baronet, had made a first, tentative approach to Erith about replacing the unsightly Victorian house on his Hertfordshire estate with one that was new, more convenient, more beautiful, but still by modern standards very large. It was the kind of job – so similar to the patronage received by a Taylor, a Chambers or a Soane – that Erith relished: 'not easy, but just the sort of thing we want,' as he wrote to Terry in January 1968. In scale and presence Kings Walden Bury was to be the most glorious of the houses by Erith. It seemed the kind of opportunity that was unlikely to come again.

By now Terry was sufficiently deeply versed in Classical architecture for his views to weigh in the discussions he and Erith would daily hold on the design. Erith remained the controlling personality, but Terry wrote the letters and drew all the details. When work started two years later, he was also persuaded by Erith's son-in-law Michael Archer, in the ceramics department of the Victoria and Albert Museum, to keep a journal recording the evolution of the house. It appeared that, as possibly the last of its kind, the house would be bound to have a certain historical importance. The record would also show people of the future how it was done. It took the form of a sketchbook called the 'Kingswalden Notes'. 'I shall keep to the part which will be of some use when modernism has collapsed,' wrote Terry in the first entry in May 1969, 'when people are in search of the secret of Classical building.'

Today there is more room for optimism about the future of country-house building in Britain. But reading the Kingswalden Notes you have a vivid sense of the dark clouds closing in round civilized values of all kinds. It is as though Terry was writing in France during the Revolution or at an outpost of the Roman Empire when the legions were pulling out. 'What a mess machine dug trenches look,' he wrote on 29 May. 'Two machines do a job badly where twenty men could do it well – still, that's progress & economy.' A percentage of Portland cement had to be used in the foundations, although, having a high degree of

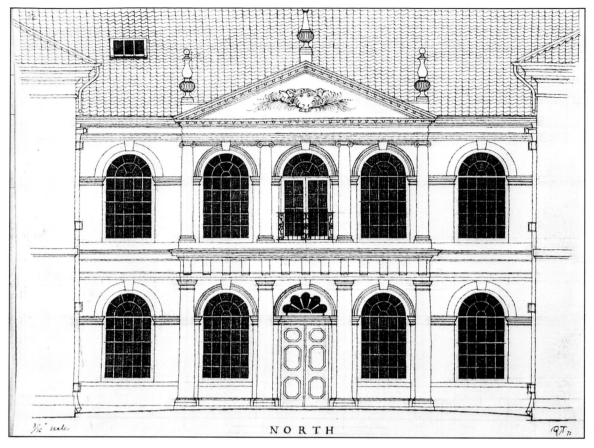

23. Kings Walden Bury: north front

thermal movement, it was a material disliked by the architects. In the past they had always used Shepreth lime, which required no cement. 'Unfortunately they have just rationalized their business & discovered that it is more profitable to sell their land for development than to manufacture lime.' The bricks came from Sudbury and were completely hand made, 'in the old way'. The same clay had been used for bricks in Roman times, but it seemed that, here again, a change was at hand: 'facing bricks have been in such a bad way recently that the son of the man who runs the works has gone over to pigs with the result that most of the kilns are full of pigs and only one is left for firing.' At times the tone is almost apocalyptic:

As I go about this Sodom; as I read my newspaper & my Bible, as I see the vileness of man coupled with the 'advances' in destructive weapons; I come to the sad but unavoidable conclusion that sooner or later mankind will destroy itself ... We must look beyond our impending destruction to a far more stable and natural world than this world has ever known. A new heaven & a new earth. We must look (like John in the Apocalypse) at that

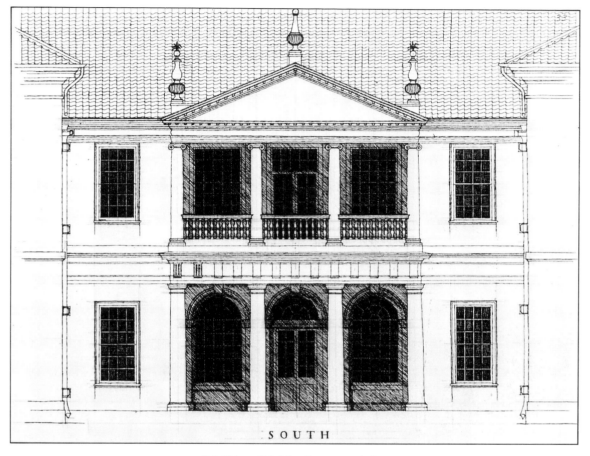

24. Kings Walden Bury: south front

great city, the holy Jerusalem, descending out of heaven from God, where the foundations are built of precious stones, the building of the wall of jasper, the gates of pearl & the streets paved with pure gold. Read it for yourself in Revelation twenty-one & elsewhere & doubt not that in that city is the perfection of all things including beauty which we in our fallen state now dimly grope after.

The physical character of the Kingswalden Notes reinforces the picture of a man of civilized instincts living through an age of barbarism. It is in the form of a sketchbook and therefore a private document which few other people could be expected to see, but the drawings in it are as exquisitely finished as an eighteenth-century engraving. Although now a Classicist, Terry was still sufficiently an Arts and Crafts man (as one might have gathered from the comment on trench digging) to spend his evening hours beneath the Lamp of Sacrifice, drawing.

The house was based closely on precedents, Palladian and English Classical, yet it fits into no pigeon-hole in the history of Italian or English architecture. As John

35

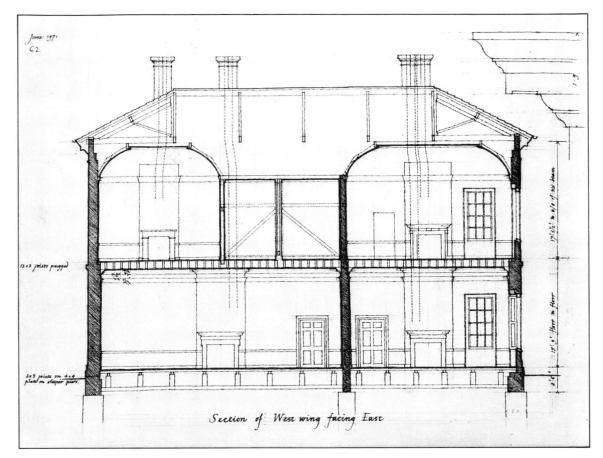

25. Kings Walden Bury: section of west wing

Cornforth observed in *Country Life*,[1] the feel is curiously like an early-eighteenth century American house such as Drayton Hall in South Carolina, which shares the double portico motif of the garden front. When you first see it from the drive or from the big sloping lawn at the back, it seems to have the same freshness and simplicity – although a closer look will show that it is far from being a simple house. From the first the principal inspiration was to be Palladio's *Quattro Libri*, but not English Palladian, because the hand-made bricks that we have already heard Terry praise were long and thin, in the Tudor fashion, and so used with wide mortar joints. The result is a softer, rougher, more rustic look than the eighteenth century would have favoured. An early Classical flavour (though seventeenth century rather than Tudor) was also suggested by the particular Doric order that the architects chose for the ground floor. 'Architecturally it is pretty

1. John Cornforth described the house in *Country Life*, 27 September and 4 October 1973.

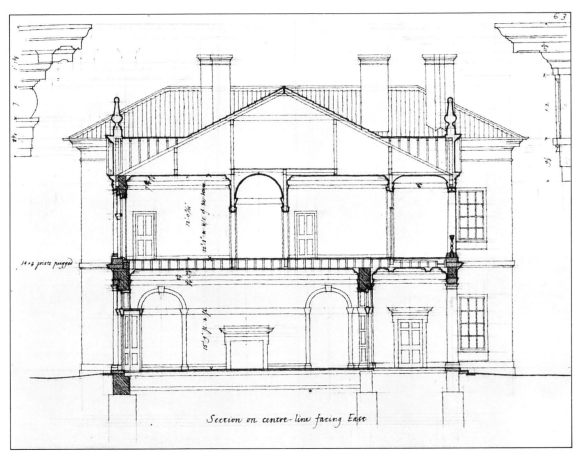

26. Kings Walden Bury: section on centre line facing east

pure Palladio,' wrote Terry. 'We imagine we have been with the master in Vicenza
& are now, like Inigo Jones, trying to spread the good news with the aid of the
Quattro Libri & very little else besides commonsense English building practice of
the period.' That was written on 13 August 1969. By 3 September the next year,
with Erith and Terry having worked intensively on the details, the character of the
house had become more involved. 'I said at the beginning that the house is really
1620,' wrote Terry. '…That idea has changed. The design has now taken the law
into its own hands & expressed a nature of its own. This is something which is
hard to describe but very much to be encouraged. On this house its nature has
turned out Baroque.'

In plan the house is an H, with a service court to the side. In the centre of the
main block is a big hall, strongly reminiscent of the Veneto. The entrance door
gives into it and faces due north. On both the north and south fronts, the wings
of the H are rather plain – flat brick, except for two pairs of square-headed

37

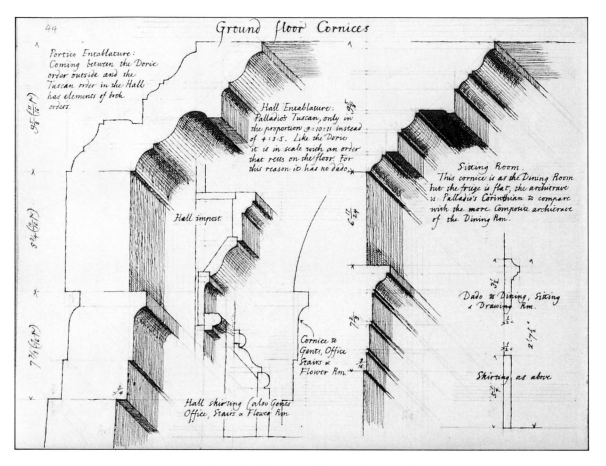

27. Kings Walden Bury: ground floor cornices

sash-windows and a projecting string course at middle and top. All the richness has been concentrated in the five bays of the centrepiece. The windows have arched heads and smaller panes, and there are all kinds of architectural 'confectionary' (Terry's word). But wait a minute: *is* the centrepiece five bays? Here we have one of the first Baroque or Mannerist complexities. For the centrepiece is really the three bays below the pediment; but the entablatures of the two orders, Doric and Ionic, have been carried through (though in a less enriched form) to include the single, order-less bays to either side. So too have the imposts and archivolts – though, again, both are plain rather than moulded. There is thus a deliberate ambiguity in the way the façade is read. Other Baroque refinements described by Terry are: 'somewhat accidentally, the roughness of the brickwork & pantile roof which, compared with the smoothness of the centrepiece give a highly textured almost vermiculated effect'; and the putting of three finials, one at each

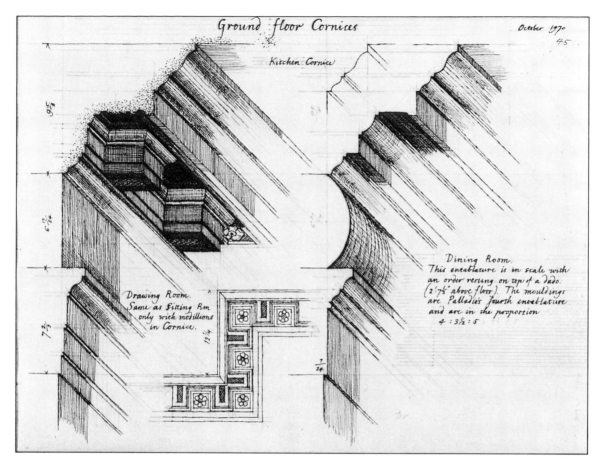

28. Kings Walden Bury: ground floor cornices

angle of the pediment, above four columns – the two outer finials being to a different design from that in the centre.

By contrast, the internal arrangement of the house is straightforward. The staircase is to one side of the big hall: it is balanced on the other side by an office and lavatory. In the west wing of the H are the drawing room and sitting room, in the east the kitchen and dining room. Simple though it appears, it also clearly makes best use of the sun. 'A preparatory sun clock related to the H shows the sun moving round from the windows of the kitchen to the dining room, which gets the sun from breakfast time until late afternoon,' wrote John Cornforth. 'The south front ... has sun throughout the middle of the day; the sitting room at the south west corner gets it from mid morning until the evening, when it also pours into the drawing room.' As for the scale of the drawing room, indeed the scale of the whole house, that was influenced by a less obvious, but fundamental, consid-

39

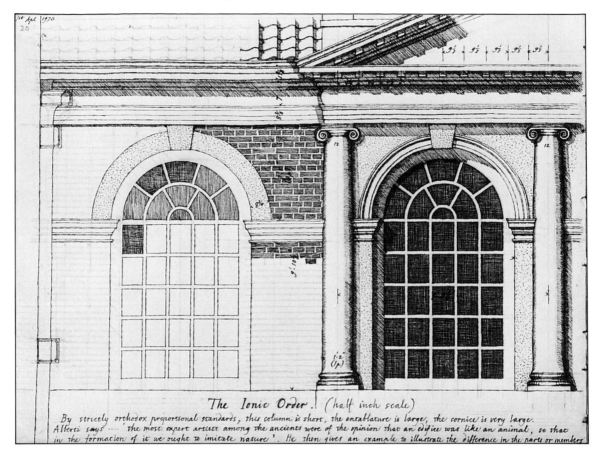

29. *Kings Walden Bury: Ionic order*

eration, in the shape of two chandeliers that the Pilkingtons already owned. These have a seven foot six inch drop, and about seven feet (seven feet one inch to be precise) were added to that length to get the ceiling height. The height in turn suggested a certain generosity for the other dimensions, the span of the wings being twenty-one feet.

But if we think in English measurements we will be lost, because the module here is not the English foot but the Venetian *piede* of 14in. The *piede* was supposed to give a more ample sense of space to the design, especially when proportions expressed as whole numbers were used. As Terry explained: 'a door three feet wide & six feet high is a good proportion (1:2) but too low to walk through; whereas three Venetian feet by six Venetian feet (3′6″ × 7′0″ English) is both comfortable and noble.' The drawing room is therefore 30p by 18p (a proportion of 5:3), the whole of the main house 81p by 54p (3:2). It was not always possible to achieve such satisfyingly simple ratios: the hall is 29p by 19p, for example, and the height

40

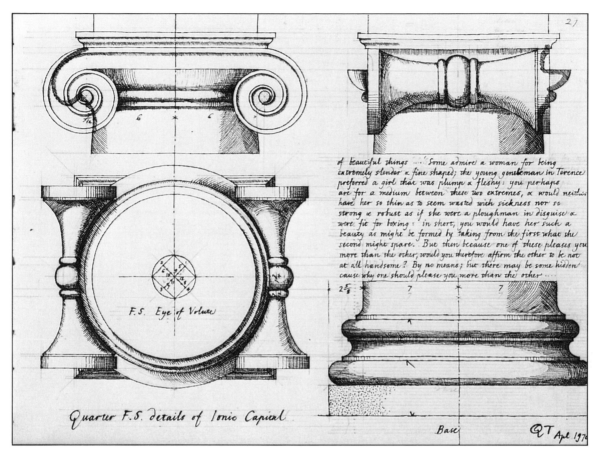

30. Kings Walden Bury: detail of Ionic capital and base

of the drawing room ceiling, at 14ft 7in, works out at 12.5p. Whether it would not have been possible to find a more satisfying expression of the more complex ratios in feet and inches is a fair question. But of course the real significance of the *piede* was not practical but symbolic: it signified the architects' great love of harmonious proportion, their equal love of the Veneto, and the time they could spend on the design. It is worth noting that, today, Terry still uses simple proportions and whole numbers wherever possible, and the *piede* has gone metric with 1080mm equalling one Venetian yard.

The Kingswalden Notes were written by an architect for practising architects. They are not anecdotal: they are concerned to explain the decisions taken in Classical architecture. The great majority of these decisions relate to the internal workings of Classicism rather than to philosophy, and most of the Notes take the form of drawings rather than words. An illustration of Erith and Terry's preoccupations lies in their Doric order. As we have seen, this was basically Palladio's –

41

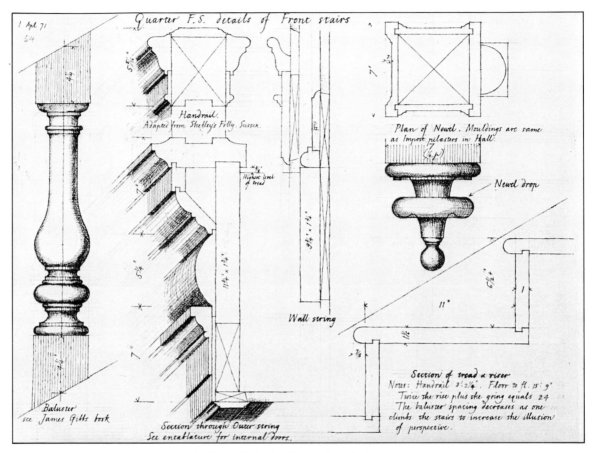

31. Kings Walden Bury: detail of staircase

but, inevitably, with modifications caused by the building. Thus, since there was only room for a slightly shorter version of the order than Palladio shows, Vignola's base was used, this being shorter than Palladio's. A cruder impost helped make it 'look more countryfied'. A smaller scale of archivolt was needed to make it fit. Following Batty Langley, the keystone was made one thirteenth of half the circumference. There were no bull's heads, and the triglyphs were altered to give a more provincial air. Even by Erith and Terry's standards, these were changes of detail. But the Ionic order was more problematical. 'I'm afraid we have not kept quite so close to the book as we did for the Doric,' wrote Terry. To explain the technicalities of the treatment it is best to quote the Kingswalden Notes *in extenso*:

The Column is 9′10⅛″ which is short. 9 times bottom diameter equals 10′6″; this column is nearer 8½D

The entablature: if architrave, frieze & cornice were 36 parts, 27 parts & 45 parts

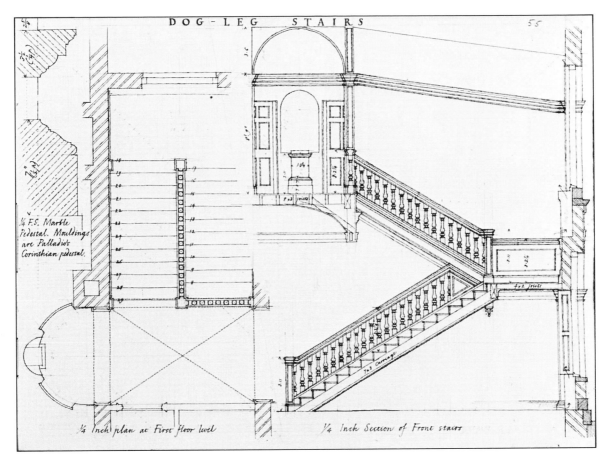

32. Kings Walden Bury: dog-leg stairs

respectively, then they would be 8⅖", 6⅔" & 10½". As you see, the architrave is about right, the frieze is a little bigger as if to anticipate the cornice which is enormous. The cornice had to be bigger, partly because of the spacing of the modillions but chiefly because it is the crowning member of the centrepiece and pediment. The spacing of the modillions is tricky. 9⅓" centres gives a centre over the column & keystone but also means a lot of projection on the bedmoulds to make the modillion on the return look right. We have got over this by using three bedmoulds instead of two & (very cunning) made the pulvinated frieze return ½" less at the top – a dodge that Palladio used on his Composite order.

It was not only the orders, the most elevated department of Classicism, that received this attention. A sash-window that seemed both pleasing to the eye and satisfied the architects' historical sense also required thought:

Look at the sketch and form your own opinion. The glazing bar is early – say Queen Anne, and yet the house is really 1620 which is pre sash window. The sill is from the

43

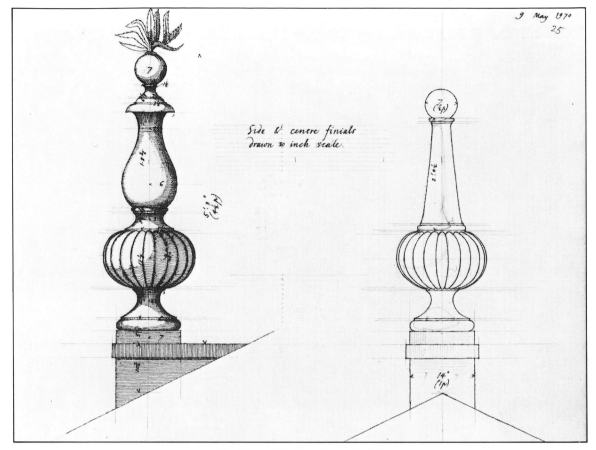

33. Kings Walden Bury: finial

village Grammar School [in Dedham] (about 1740). It looks like a Dutch sash where the box is solid with a groove cut out for the weights & yet the construction is English. The outer lining is very thick & really gives more the impression of an architrave than a sash box. These apparent contradictions might shock some historians, yet I am sure traditional architects have always felt free to take a leaf out of anybodies [sic] book to suit the needs of their time.

Clearly the complications are considerable and likely in some cases to be over-looked by people who are not practising Classical architects – or at least gentlemen amateurs in the eighteenth-century tradition. To play the history game you cannot just go straight off to the cribs. You have to decide which is the right crib. When you have got there, it is probable that the crib will provide only part of the information you need. If you turn to one of the seventeenth-century Italian masters, for example – and there is always the matter of which one you choose – you will find that they show the proportions of the orders with the profiles of their mouldings, but not all that much else. In the case of Palladio, there

are no directions given about the scale or the spacing of the columns or the snags of spacing triglyphs & metopes between them. One is not told when one can alter the rules to achieve an effect & when one can't. There is no guidance about the pros & cons of half engaged columns as against three quarter engaged & their use with pilasters & so forth. But not only is there no information about the way to handle an order or a moulding; there is no indication of the construction. If it is to be in stone one has to decide on the size of each stone & how they will be supported. If it is in timber, a separate set of rules apply regarding shrinkage & bracketting & weathering. If the construction is not genuine & traditional the effect will soon be apparent & that effect will be appallingly amateur.

Then there is the further question, which can only be one of eye coupled with experience, of how different sources may be mixed to solve the particular problems of the building being designed. Terry's conclusion was typical: 'It all points to the fact that among the many qualifications necessary to be an architect, one must also be middle-aged!'

8 The Doric Order.

The dimensions are given in English & Venetian (where it is significant) in parts related to the bottom diameter.

The bases, imposts, caps, architraves & cornices are in worked Portland stone. The shafts are made up of 2" thick stone discs built in to course with the brickwork. It is then plastered. The architraves on the South side span from column to column in one stone. On the North, the centre of the architrave is built into the brickwork as a keystone in reverse, thus halving the span between the columns.

Architecturally it is pretty pure Palladio. We imagine we have been with the master in Vicenza & are now, like Inigo Jones, trying to spread the good news with the aid of the Quattro Libri & very little else besides commonsense English building practice of the period; this incidentally is a key to the brickwork. But to return to the Quattro Libri. If you turn to his Doric Order you will see the similarities. We have only wavered for reasons of necessity, not originality; which is of course excusable. They are as follows :-. Vignola's base being shorter helps to counteract the shortness of the shaft. 2. A coarser impost to help it look more countrified & because we wanted to use the Doric impost upstairs.

34. Kings Walden Bury: Doric order

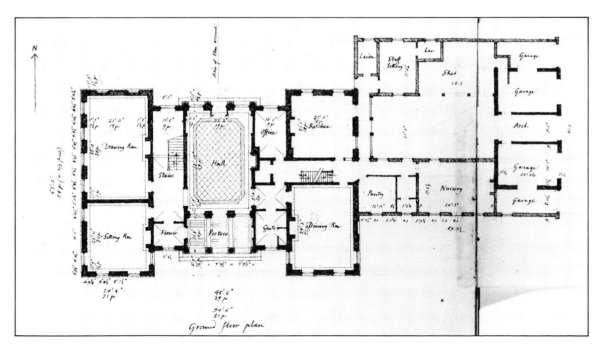

35. Kings Walden Bury: ground floor plan

37. Kings Walden Bury: first floor plan (facing)

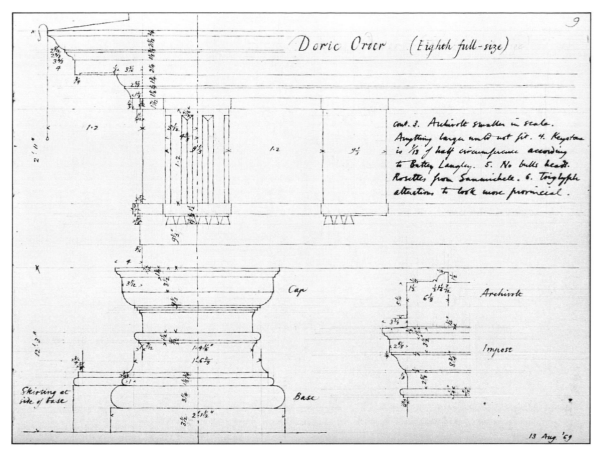

36. *Kings Walden Bury: detail of Doric order*

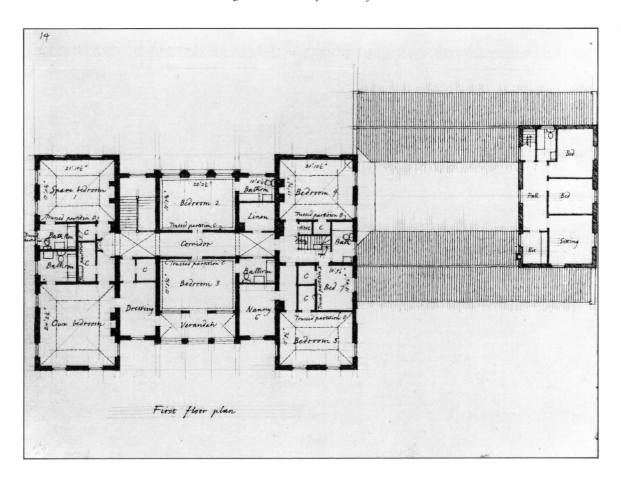

38. Kings Walden Bury: north front

39. Kings Walden Bury: south front (facing)

40. Kings Walden Bury: hall

41. Kings Walden Bury: staircase (facing)

42. The temple: elevation of main entrance

CHAPTER FIVE

THE TEMPLE

Some eighteen months before his death Erith was approached about a commission which was to provide the office with five years' continuous work and perhaps ensure its survival when his personal leadership was gone, and when the oil crisis had shaken the confidence of private clients. Had it been built it would have proved one of the most spectacular undertakings of twentieth-century architecture. But it would probably also have engrossed Terry's time and attention to such an extent that he might well have built nothing else to date.

The commission was for a temple or House of Worship for the Baha'i religion on a site near Tehran. The introduction came through the big civil engineering firm of Ove Arup and Partners, who had already done the structural design of an important monument in Iran – the Shahyad Memorial – which had been designed by a Baha'i. Like the Jewish religion in Europe, the Baha'i faith numbers an unusually high percentage of the commercial, entrepreneurial and educated classes among its adherents. But again like Judaism it has a history of persecution, and was only marginally more acceptable to the last Iranian regime than it is to the present. Despite the unfavourable political climate, the Baha'is were determined to press ahead with their temple. For they believe that they have received the divine message to unify mankind, and this is symbolized by the construction of great buildings with domes. These temples are the centre for a whole cluster of other institutions providing medical and other care for the community. By 1973 the Baha'is had acquired the site. Although they had not been able to obtain permission to build on it, they intended to move ahead a little at a time in the hope they would not actually be stopped.

The faith was founded by a nineteenth-century religious teacher called Bahaullah. It is a world faith which acknowledges the divine origin of all the great religions. The teachings of the Prophet were fostered and disseminated by his eldest son Abdul Baha and by the latter's grandson Shoghi Effendi Rabbani, who succeeded him as head of the faith in 1921. (By coincidence Shoghi Effendi had been at Balliol with Terry's uncle.) In the 1950s Shoghi Effendi had requested the

44. *The temple: Quinlan Terry and Raymond Erith on the site*

45. *The temple: the first design, side elevation*

43. *The temple: elevation of the first design (facing)*

46. *The temple: the site*

American architect Charles Mason Remey, who was himself a Baha'i, to design a temple in Tehran. Mason Remey, already an old man, was only able to draw three sketches – a plan, an elevation and a section – before his death. There was no detailed scale. But the Baha'is are people of great piety towards their past and the Mason Remey design, with its association with Shogi Effendi, was held to be sacrosanct. Their devotion to history appealed greatly to Erith, at a time when it seemed that nothing was held to be sacred in England.

Erith and Terry first went out to Iran, at their own expense, in April 1972. Four other architects had been invited to quote: one Iranian, one French and two Italian. Erith told the Baha'is that he had been waiting all his life to work on a job of this kind, and they were won over by such a piece of enthusiasm and humility from a man whom they believed to be a great architect. It was at first to be a three-year contract and the quotation was based on the annual running costs of the office, plus a margin. Erith and Terry were awarded the commission; eastern courtesies were exchanged; and the architects returned to England to translate Mason Remey's design into, for Erith's peace of mind, the language of Classicism.

The great strength of Mason Remey's design had been that, with his Beaux-Arts training, he had been able to tease out the numerical complexities required by the Baha'is. Nine and nineteen are mystical numbers to the Baha'is: nine symbolizing perfection as well as the Baha'i faith itself (there are nine ways to God), nineteen being an emblem of unity as the numerical value of the letters composing the Arab word for unit. So nine and nineteen recur throughout the design, and as neither is divisible by the other this was a source of endless conflicts in the mathematics. Not all of these had been resolved in the sketch plans. For instance, while there are nineteen windows in the clerestory of the dome, the latter is supported on nine piers. How could a satisfying spacing of windows over piers be achieved? Erith found the answer by thickening the two piers facing the entrance arch. By this means each bay could have two windows apiece except the bay at the front, which had three. Although otherwise traditionalists in both work and life, Erith and Terry were glad of the invention of the calculator which greatly helped with the long division by nineteen and the trigonometrical readings for chords.

Mason Remey's design allowed for a great central space surrounded by roughly semi-circular chapels. Externally the temple was to be dominated by a dome of immense size: the dome of Terry's final design would, if built, have the same diameter as Les Invalides in Paris and only five feet less than that of St Paul's. In their first design Erith and Terry intended that the dome should be of load-bearing construction. The low curve of the profile was essentially Italianate, and there was

56

a cornice with a balustrade. The windows in the clerestory were round-headed. Mason Remey's minarets were interpreted somewhat as Siennese towers. The entrance was to be through a Bramante-esque tripartite arch. In front of it was a grand Renaissance double sweep of steps.

When Erith and Terry went back to Iran in April 1973, the Baha'is' response to their work was that, frankly, they were depressed by it. They did not want the Mason Remey design to be taken as a starting point, they wanted it to be adhered to *exactly*. This seemed almost too much for Erith to suffer. An aspect of Mason Remey's design was that it had expressed the composite nature of the Baha'i faith in architecture: it took what might be thought of as the best elements of the different traditions of architecture throughout the world and blended them in a way that seemed quite unacceptable to a scholar and purist like Erith. Terry, however, was less appalled. At nearly seventy Erith did not have to think quite so minutely about future plans as his young partner. The realities of the situation seemed, bluntly, that it was better to work conscientiously on detailing the Mason Remey design than to give up architecture in Dedham and take a job with, for instance, the GLC.

And there was more to it than merely practical considerations. Terry is sympathetic to the Picturesque tradition in a way that Erith, with his rationalism, never was. Mixing styles in the same composition did not seem impossible, and we may perhaps see in his acquiescence to the Baha'is' demands for eclecticism a foretaste of the Richmond Riverside development, where the principle of Picturesque contrast has been used to avoid monotony in long terraces. Terry also finds that, in any design, it is the working-out of problems of detail that perhaps gives more pleasure than anything else. The difficulty for Terry lay more in the Baha'is' attempt to merge religions than in their attempt to merge styles. As the commission wore on he was to have doubts about the morality of a Christian designing a place of worship for an alien faith. The anxiety at one point caused him, unusually, a sleepless night, and he was only reassured by a talk with the Welsh preacher Gwyn Thomas, whom Terry valued highly as a guide. It was his last meeting with Thomas, who died unexpectedly a week later.

Largely for Terry's sake Erith consented to rework the design, but he died before this second design was truly underway. In the second design Islamic arches were married with Classical columns throughout the building, and a similar convergence of cultures is expressed in the dome. The Baha'is had asked for a combination of the Taj Mahal – an Eastern dome, with the characteristic swelling silhouette – and St Peter's – a Western dome with cornice and lantern. The

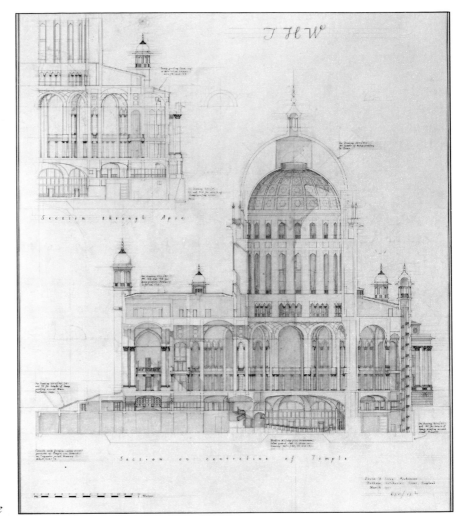

47. *The temple: section on centre line*

48. *The temple: south elevation*

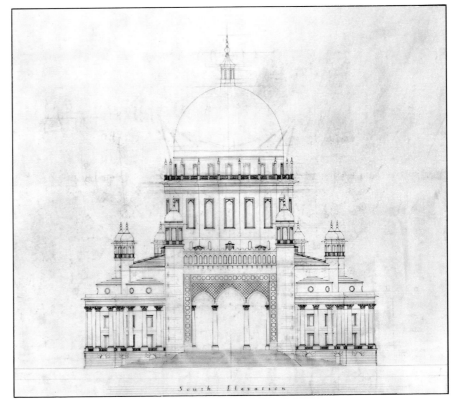

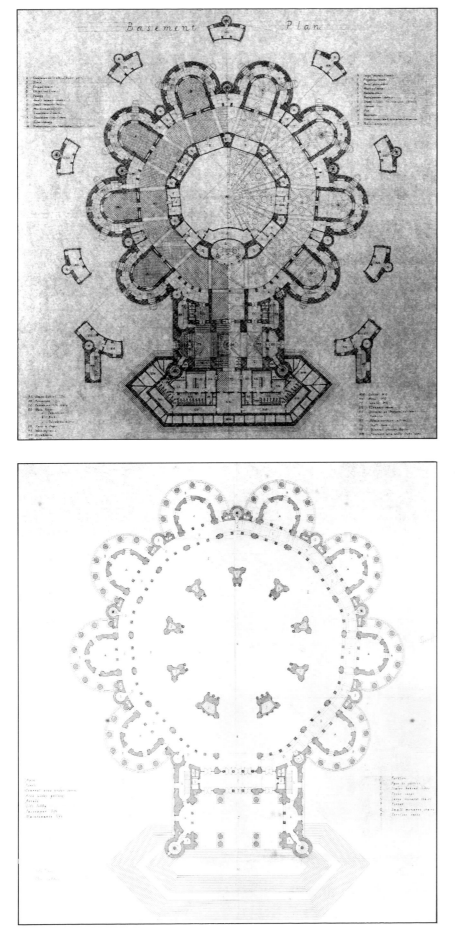

49. *The temple: basement plan*

50. *The temple: ground floor plan*

resulting compromise, which had rarely been tried before (perhaps the only previous occasion being the Baha'is' Shrine of the Bab in Haifa), was far less unhappy than one might have predicted. Terry was fortunate in winning the Sir Herbert Baker scholarship while he was at work on the temple and this enabled him to undertake a study of dome construction. The sketchbook in which his findings are recorded begins charmingly: 'I went to see Mr L. A. Minter on October 21st 1972 at his house at Bulmer, Sudbury, Suffolk to ask him how he made his domed brick kiln, which he built in 1936. I also measured it.' It would have been some way from Mr Minter's kiln to a building the size of the temple. The sketchbook also contains, in the preface, the typical observation that the 'few people who have been able to help me are either octogenarian or dead'. On Friday, 13 April 1973, Erith and Terry were taken to the Mausoleum of Uljaitu at Sultanijeh, which has an egg-shaped brick dome. It was both under scaffolding and closed for the Moslem rest day: this combination of factors enabled Erith to measure the plan and Terry the section.

Designing a building on the scale of the temple was a superb exercise in geometry – even if the architect has yet to see how his spaces work out in practice. It gave Terry immense experience of designing detail: there are, for instance, four or five versions of Corinthian capital in the temple, one of them taken from a type illustrating the supposed origin of the order (a basket around which an acanthus plant grew) found in Jerusalem. For the balustrades and splendid geometrical floor patterns (marble was to have been used throughout) Terry tended to look to Venice: the Venice both of Byzantium and of the Baroque. It is of course in Venice, supremely, that Eastern and Western traditions merge. Immense pains had to be taken to cope with the nine- and nineteen-sided spaces; and two months were spent detailing the elliptical staircase that was to have swept down to the basement meeting hall. (The last was an afterthought of the clients. It would have had to have been equipped with all the technology of a United Nations-style simultaneous-translation conference room, since, the Baha'i faith being world-wide, it was expected that worshippers would come from all countries and would speak many languages.)

Style, however, was only one of the ways in which the second design differed radically from the first. In the time between the two, Arups had insisted that, as the building was to lie on an earthquake fault, the structure had to be of reinforced concrete. This gave Terry a first-hand introduction to the problems of the material, which convinced him to use it as little as possible henceforth. In order that the soft expansion joints – necessary to accommodate creep and thermal movement – should not obtrude, it was decided that the whole of the masonry should be rusticated. However, the concrete construction would not have been entirely without benefit, since it provided hollow spaces in the piers that could be used for service ducts. The servicing for the temple had to be at a very high level. In the desert temperatures air-conditioning was essential. One of the great lessons of the temple was how the mechanical services can be concealed within the architecture. Classicism, being highly articulated, is particularly well adapted for this. Corinthian columns can enrich a space while also concealing air conditioning ducts and grilles. It should also be said that Mason Remey's Beaux-Arts design was highly inefficient in its use of space: it therefore provided enormous voids in which to hide chillers and other service plant.

All the drawings necessary to build the temple were made and they are now with members of the Baha'i religion in different parts of the world. Work ceased (for the time being, at least) when the site, together with all other properties and holy places of the Baha'i community in Iran, was confiscated during the current wave of persecutions which started in 1979. But there is no doubt that, whenever times allow, and however far that may be in the future, the temple will be built. It was, and is, the Baha'is' object to construct the temple piece by piece, as circumstances allowed; the drawings were designed to this end. Thus, should a rich donor appear on the scene he might, for instance, pay for all the Corinthian capitals, which would then be stored. It also seems likely that, whether or not Terry himself is involved, it will be built as closely to Terry's design as Terry was constrained to follow Mason Remey's. So we may yet see the vast dome rise above the barren foothills of the Elburz mountains, and the enormous encircling parterres that Terry also planned may still make the desert flower. In the meantime, as a memento, Terry can produce from his wallet a photograph of the Pharaoh-like excavations for the foundations: all that had been executed before the Peacock Throne fell.

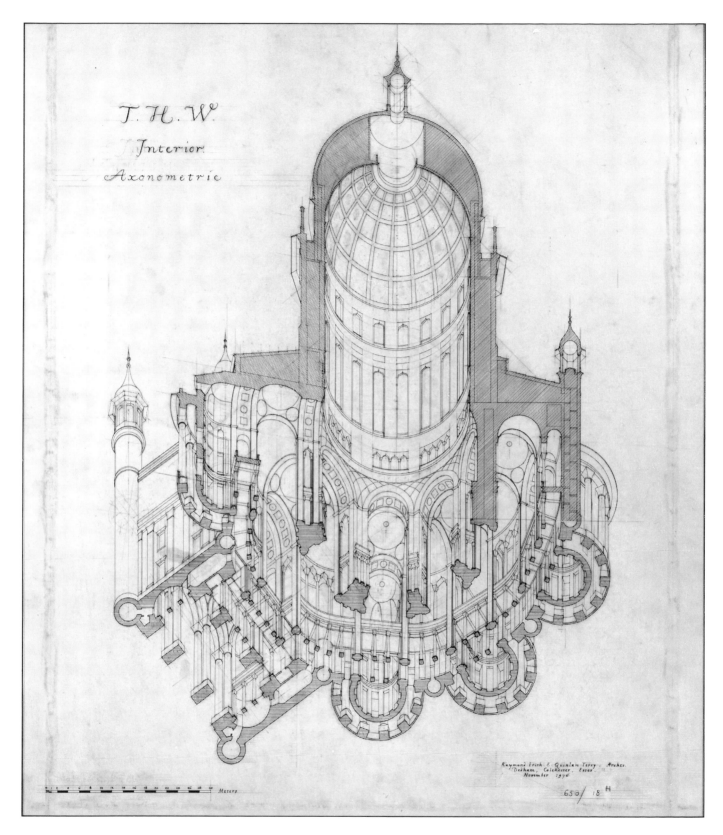

52. The temple: axonometric of interior

51. The temple: elevation of the dome (facing)

FROG

House no 5 built 1979

r. Sc. PL. Imp.

53 and 54. Front door and porch, Winterfloods (see page 20)
55. Frog Meadow: detail of linocut

CHAPTER SIX

LITTLE HOUSES

The temple was a heroic project on the grandest scale, but the list of works at the end of this book shows that the mainstay of the Erith and Terry practice has been jobs of a different kind. Roof repairs, alterations to doors and windows, the construction of bathroom extensions and garden buildings: this was the sort of work that was actually being done while the temple was being designed. It reflects oddly on the idea that Classical architecture only works for big, prestige commissions; that your client needs to be a millionaire.

'How would you deal with the problem of the ordinary man in the street?' complained the architect Brian Cox at the end of a talk by Terry to the Royal Institute of British Architects in November 1982. To him, Terry's architecture seemed 'totally unrealistic and uneconomic in our present day world'. According to this argument, which already has a strangely dated ring, Classicism is all right for country houses but not for offices, small houses and so on. The variety of Terry's practice shows up the misapprehension. It is not just that he has in the last few years received three major commissions for office buildings (see Chapters 9 and 12). Even in the domestic sphere he has built for clients of all means, and the budget has sometimes been modest. Some of the work would probably have been beneath the notice of a big Modernist office. One suspects that few of the critics who call him impractical have ever built a house of seven hundred square feet, as the Erith and Terry practice has done at Frog Meadow in Dedham. Country houses stand at the top of the architectural hierarchy, but no less interesting, particularly at a time when the Classical Revival is becoming widespread, are the buildings at the other end of the scale.

Frog Meadow is a row of seven houses, some single and some attached, which turn the corner at the eastern entrance to the village. It was begun in 1966. Previously, when it was first known that the site had been given outline planning permission, Erith and Terry feared that an illiterate speculative development would be slapped down on their own doorstep. Dedham was deeply important to Erith and is still to Terry. If it has survived as one of the loveliest villages in

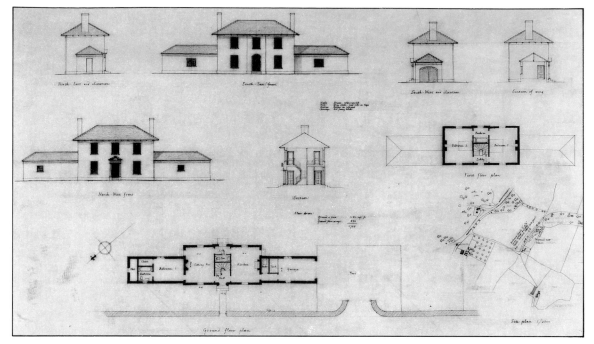

56. House near Penn's in the Rocks, 1973 (unbuilt)

England, completely unspoilt by modern intrusions, that is no accident. Erith felt the ugliness of the modern world almost physically, like something gnawing at his stomach. He was a passionate conservationist and would rush out of his office and frighten away the council employees who had come to erect road signs or paint white lines – perhaps by demanding if they had a faculty. Terry has inherited Erith's campaigning spirit. The building of the public lavatory could not be stopped (public lavatories are an evil, Terry believes, because they encourage charabancs), but it is sited so far down a footpath that it does not detract from the High Street, and only the best-rehearsed tour operators would know it was there. Ironically there would have been no public lavatory and no coach tours if Erith, Terry and those of like mind had not fought to protect Dedham from the modern world. The wrong development at Frog Meadow would have been an affront to everything Erith and Terry had fought to preserve.

Fortunately, however, a generous-spirited local resident stepped in to buy the land and Erith and Terry were asked to design houses for it. These were to be built one by one, starting at the eastern end and working along, as and when clients appeared. So it was fourteen years before the full complement of houses was completed. They were built to different designs; a development to one design would have seemed overwhelming to the rest of the village. The old shops and houses of Dedham – almost every one of which has been repaired or altered by Erith and Terry over the years – are not of a uniform size or style. They vary from the tiniest weatherboarded cottages to Sherman's House, an early eighteenth-century brick Classical building owned formerly by the 1930s Classical architect Marshall Sisson and now by the National Trust. But, together with the big East Anglian church, the total effect of the different buildings is harmonious, because they were all built by traditional methods, using natural and largely local materials. Frog Meadow was designed to fit in with this texture.

With his enthusiasm for instant history Erith liked the notion of a development in assorted styles, and the Picturesque concept of diversity within unity is one that Terry finds naturally attractive. We have seen it in the Baha'i temple (Chapter 5); it will be developed at Richmond Riverside (Chapter 12). Yet it would be missing the point to make too much of the Frog Meadow houses. As Terry writes: 'They are not high grade buildings, just a rank and file continuation of the village street, using typical Essex vernacular detail of plain and pantile roofs, wide and narrow glazing bars on sash and casement windows, brickwork in flemish bond, stucco, and a slight variation in doorcases.'[1] The style is not so much Classical in the grand sense as what would now be called vernacular: the style of a country builder working within the constraints of a tradition.

The differences in design are best seen in Terry's two linocuts, which also give the dates at which each house was built. But as you walk down the pavement on the other side of the street you do not take in the full span at a glance, especially when the leaves are out on

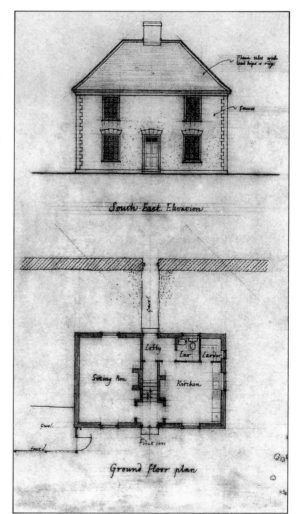

57. *House near Penn's in the Rocks, 1973*

1. *Architectural Design*, 3–4, 1979, p.109.

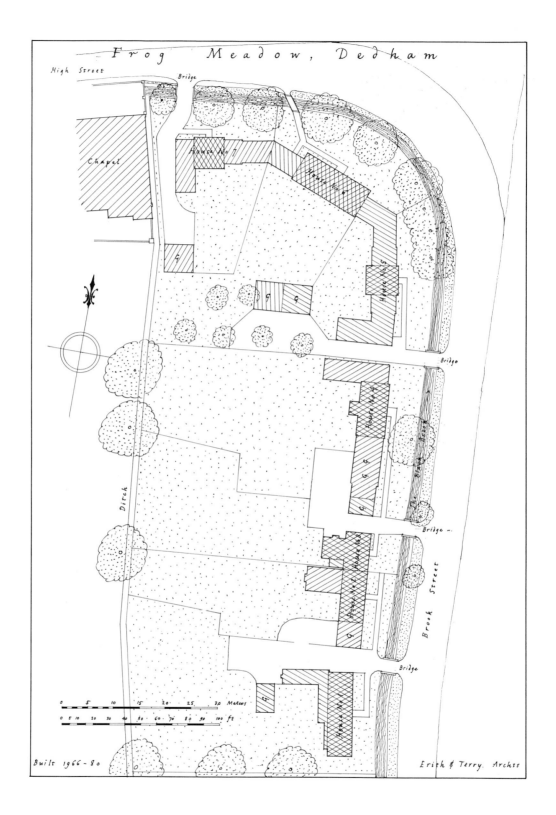

58. Frog Meadow: plan

the trees. You see only two or three houses together. So the variations do not become irritating or seem contrived.

The first three houses were designed by Erith, Terry continuing the scheme with Nos. 4 to 7 after his death. No.1 Frog Meadow is also the largest: five bays wide and stuccoed, with sash-windows downstairs, a decent door-case, a plain tiled roof and plaster quoins. These seemingly simple things are not so simple to achieve, given that country builders are more likely to rely on catalogues than on craftsmen for details. All the details in the Frog Meadow houses had to be drawn out full-size. And it is not really as simple as it looks at first glance. The two ground-floor windows to the left of the door and the one immediately over it are blind. Why? Because Erith's elder sister, Barbara, for whom this was built, had a large mahogany bookcase which she wished to fit into the drawing room. This required a long expanse of blank wall.

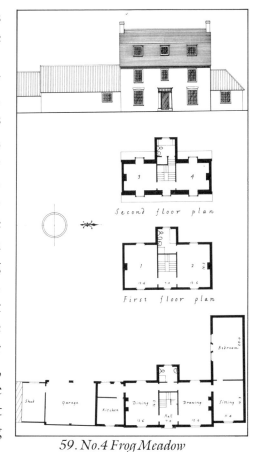

59. No.4 Frog Meadow

The garden front is rambling compared to that of the street. This is typical of numerous village houses which put a neat face to the world but are seen in unbuttoned mood at the back, where sensible arrangements are made for service rooms. But, equally, the back of No.1 is not without its show of elegance, possessing two circular windows to either side of the big, circular-headed window over the stairs. The garden window of the drawing room, which, having no outlook to the street, needs plenty of light from this side, was based on the old shop window of Erith and Terry's office. The budget was less restricted here than for some of the other Frog Meadow houses.

No.2 Frog Meadow is a very simple building, and No.3 which is attached to it, simpler still. Like No.1, the plan of No.2 is L-shaped, but here with the main room – a music room – at the back. The couple for whom the house was built were retired and felt that two bedrooms were adequate. So the house takes the form of a plain two-up, two-down, with an extension at the back. The street elevation is only three bays across. It is brick with a pantile roof and sash-windows, and the

minimally Classical doorcase (a more attenuated version of No.1's) is perhaps the only detail to look out of
the ordinary. The door gives into a little hall – only six
feet nine inches wide – which has the stairs going up
and around it at the back. On the left of the building is
the garage: with faultless consideration for neighbours
and passers-by, all the garages in Frog Meadow face
the garden, so that the double doors do not disrupt the
pattern of the street.

No.3 is the seven hundred square foot house – just
over one thousand square foot if you count the garage.
It is not, to be fair, quite as run of the mill as the size
would suggest, because the owner, Joan Durrant, was
an assistant in the Erith and Terry office. It would have
been a typical Erith tease, had he been able to foresee
the way the rest of the designs would go, that this, the
tiniest of the Frog Meadow houses, should be the only
one with a pediment. It may seem an affectation in
such a small building. But as Terry commented in
International Architect,[2] these signs of sophistication
are a true reflection of the way the village has changed
socially. Cottages are no longer lived in by farm lab-
ourers, but by professional people. 'For this reason
there is inevitably more Architecture per cubic foot.' It
is an indication that traditional, country-builder's
Classicism is a living and evolving style. The key to the
success of the design was that the owner went for
quality of finish rather than size of rooms.

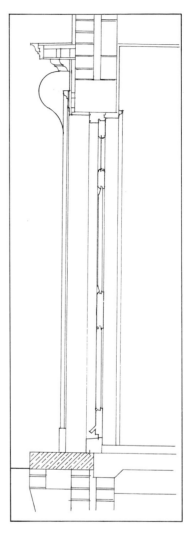

*60. No.5 Frog Meadow: front
door (detail of Figure 61)*

The first house designed by Terry alone, No.4, has a gambrel roof similar to that
of two farmhouses on the other side of the road. The roof has dormers, and is a
means of accommodating extra space for bedrooms without making the house
seem unduly tall. Again, there is more to this house than at first meets the eye: the
sash-windows, for example, are of varying sizes, and so are the dormers. It may
seem that this burdens a relatively little building with too much design, but it
gives life to the façade. No.4 is also the first of the Frog Meadow houses to have
a complete order to the doorcase. It is a delectable building – although, because of

2. Volume 1, No.6, 1981.

the client's changes of mind, the original clarity of the plan has become somewhat muddied by two extensions at the back.

For the final three houses, Nos. 5 to 7, the method of building was different from the others. They were not designed for individual clients but for a speculator. It was precisely to avoid a speculative development that the original, piecemeal way of working had been adopted. But of course it depends on the speculator, and in this case he was prepared to fall in with the spirit of Frog Meadow as it had developed so far. That the last three plots were in a single ownership also had a positive advantage, from Terry's point of view. These plots are the three on the angle of the road. They occupy, therefore, a prominent position as the full stop of the village. Terry felt that a slightly grander effect was called for than in Nos. 1 to

61. Frog Meadow: doorway of Nos. 5 and 7

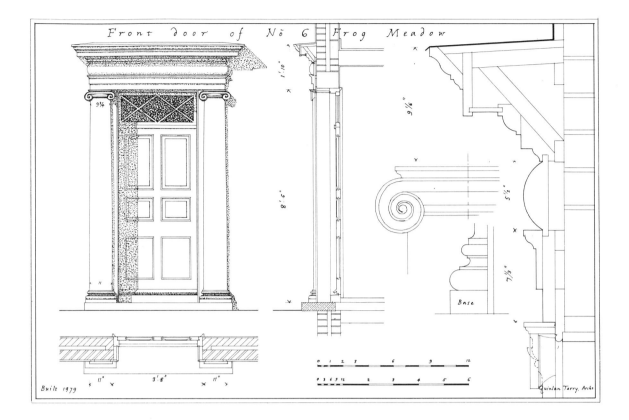

62. No.6 Frog Meadow: front door

4. Because he was working for a single client he was able to unite the three buildings in one composition, conceived on the lines of a Palladian country house as a central block with flanking wings. This treatment was particularly satisfactory since the additional sense of architectural presence is achieved at little extra relative cost.

For the wings to be in proportion with the not enormous main block, they had to seem like little lodges. You cannot imagine that the wings could provide sufficient accommodation to satisfy a modern middle-class buyer – even if, as had been thought, the buyer was retired or possibly single. The elevations are, loosely speaking, triangular, with only a single window to the first floor. But astonishingly the first, No.5, contains a sitting room, dining room, kitchen, study, dressing room and three bedrooms; No.7, the same, minus only the study. The answer to this Tardis-like puzzle is that they both make use of the screen wall by which they are linked to No.6.

The lodge doorcases are flanked by brackets, and the architrave, frieze and cornice are six, five and seven inches – in other words, in simple numerical proportion. The doorcase of No.6 is Ionic. Above it is a niche and urn in *trompe-l'œil*: not a Dedham characteristic but a visual trick much enjoyed by Terry (see Chapter 8). Here he uses it precisely as it would have been in Rome: as a cheap means of achieving an effect that would have been too expensive in three dimensions. The arch of the niche is reflected in the hood of the dormer in the roof.

The *trompe-l'œil* indicates the degree to which Nos. 5 to 7 are no longer in the village vernacular as Nos. 1 to 4 had been. Contemporary with No.6 are three much bigger projects – the restoration of Auchinleck in Ayrshire, Waverton House in Gloucestershire and the design of Newfield in Yorkshire. They all show Terry exploring different treatments of the five-bay façade. No.6 Frog Meadow looks ahead to the country houses of the next chapter.

THE HERMITAGE

Despite their occasional caprice, the Frog Meadow houses derive from the practical school of village building. The Hermitage, by contrast, belongs to a different tradition – that of the *cottage orné*. It is eminently 'the cottage appropriate to the residence of a gentleman', as the architect Edmund Bartell described one of his designs in 1804.[3] The name 'The Hermitage' itself suggests the Regency, and the location – in the park of a much larger house in north Dorset – is, appropriately, one of rural quietude. At first sight it might appear strange to include The Hermitage in a chapter on little houses; but in size it is not really all that big. It only seems so at first because of the very happy plan and the quality of the workmanship. The accommodation is all on one floor. And you could not mistake it for a Regency building. In the Regency *cottage orné*, simplicity was an affectation and few architects could resist over-egging the custard in their enthusiasm for rustic motifs. But, very pretty though it is, The Hermitage does not cross the border into fantasy. There is a sense of restraint about it; a genuine simplicity. This restraint reflects the taste of the client as much as that of the architect.

First, the origins of the design. Initially it had been hoped to convert an abandoned dairy of about 1830 which stood on the site. But when the roof was taken off, the walls collapsed and it was decided to build completely from new. The idea of the dairy, however, provided the theme for the present house. The

3. In *Hints for Picturesque Improvements in Ornamental Cottages and their Scenery*.

walls of the drawing room, the largest room of the house, stand roughly where those of the dairy had been. The room projects at right angles from the long front range, as though the dairy had been retained and the front range was an addition. Also the dairy's coved ceiling is reflected in that of the drawing room.

One might think, too, that the feel of the dairy had been retained in the materials – and it could well have been so, for the materials are both decorative and vernacular. But in fact the dairy had been built out of poor-quality brick and stucco, and the roof, though thatched, was in bad order. Thatch was, however, a requirement of the owner, who had always wanted to live under a thatched roof. It was also his choice that the thatchers did not execute any fancy patterns to the ridge. The walls are of brick and flint, in bands. These are local building materials

63. The Hermitage (linocut)

and visits were made to a church in the neigh-
bourhood to see how the courses should be
arranged. But the design is lifted above the
vernacular by Portland stone quoins – for this is,
after all, a gentleman's house. Whereas the dairy
had had pointed Gothick windows, rectangular
casements were decided upon for The Hermitage. At all points whimsy is kept in check.

The chimneystack thrusts up from the side of
the 'old dairy' wing, as this is where the fireplace is. Consequently it is off-centre in the long
stretch of roof at the front. But reflecting the
chimney to the other side, and adding another
note in the composition, is a louvre in teak and
lead which conceals the soil pipes. To those
people – and there are some – who might be less
than sure about this detail, one might quote
Lugar, writing of a *cottage orné* in *The Country
Gentleman's Architect*: 'the fastidious should be
disarmed of the severity of criticism, when the
picturesque and the useful are conveniently and
pleasingly united'.

You enter the house directly into a stone-
flagged oval hall with a domed ceiling. The shape
was a requirement of the client, who had an oval
dining table. Again, the room is not large but
feels bigger than it is because of the handsome
conception. An advantage of the oval shape is
that Terry could use the corners formed with the
rectangle in which it is contained to hide four

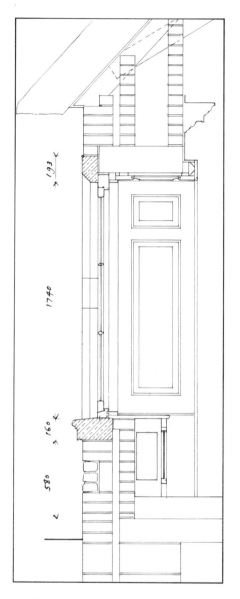

64. *The Hermitage: detail of window*

useful rooms: cloakroom, boiler room, flower room and laundry room. The
geometry is that of, in Erith's term, the Pythagorean oval, which has four centres
– arranged on the points of a diamond, itself made up of four 5-4-3 triangles – and
two radii. A true ellipse with many centres would be impossible to dimension. On
the opposite side of the hall from the front door, a door gives into the drawing
room – occupying roughly the volume of the old dairy (though the dairy was
divided up into several rooms). This has window seats and shutters at the client's

request, and at the far, south-east end a French window opening onto the terrace. From the windows you look onto the cedars and lake of the park. There is a fireplace but also underfloor heating, which runs throughout the house.

Here you are in the short upright stroke of the T plan; let us return to the hall for the long cross arm. If you open the doors there is a long enfilade through the whole length of the house. This is an enjoyable but accidental effect, and in fact somewhat contrary to the genius of the design. For what makes The Hermitage so convenient is the way the different elements of living have been isolated. At one end are the client's own rooms: bedroom, closets, study, bathroom. At the other end is the guest suite of bedroom and bathroom, which can be closed off and little heated when not in use. Then next to the hall is the big kitchen – which is really, after the hall and the dining room, the third living room of the house. The furniture, in ash, makes it a happy counterpart to the other rooms; but there is also a separate entrance – French windows onto the terrace – for when it is in use for dinner parties. The client insisted on having a step down from the hall, which provides a little variety of floor level in a house without stairs – and nicely suggests just the right degree of hierarchy of function. The hierarchy is self-imposed, however, for The Hermitage was designed to be manageable as far as possible without domestic help.

65. No.6 Frog Meadow, Dedham

House no 1. built 1967   House no 2. built 1969   Ho

Q T. SC. PL. Imp.

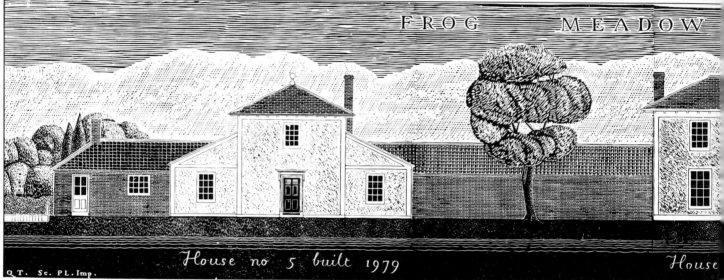

House no 5 built 1979   House

Q T. Sc. PL. Imp.

66. Frog Meadow (linocut)

67. No.5 Frog Meadow

68. No.3 Frog Meadow,
the 700 square foot house (facing)

DEDHAM · ESSEX

built 1972   House no 4 built 1977

ERITH & TERRY ARCHTS. DEDHAM. MCMLXXX

DEDHAM   ESSEX

built 1979   House no 7 being built 1980

ERITH & TERRY ARCHTS. DEDHAM. MCMLXX

70. *No.6 Frog Meadow*

69. *No.4 Frog Meadow (facing)*

71. *The Hermitage*

72. Little Roydon Hall: carved capital from the porch

CHAPTER SEVEN

THE COUNTRY HOUSES

At the time it seemed as though Kings Walden Bury might well be the last house of its size with which Terry would be involved in designing. The oil crisis shook the confidence of people likely to build country houses, and the escalation of building costs combined with rumours of a wealth tax under the Labour government seemed prohibitive. More than most human activities, the building of a country house implies a faith that the future will be recognizably like today. To sink a large sum of money in raising a house or in planting trees, which may not mature for thirty or fifty years, you must believe that you and your family will continue to be associated with the one spot that you have chosen for a considerable length of time – perhaps, you may hope, for more than your own lifetime. 'If you've got a lot of money, what nicer thing can you do with it than to build a house?' Terry has been quoted as saying.[1] 'You could spend it on a yacht or a racehorse, which is very temporary. But if you build a house, it's a monument to this age, to what you think of. And it goes on for your son and grandson.' With or without due reason, belief in continuity has been considerably strengthened by the general elections of 1979 and 1983, and Terry is busy with more country houses than could have been predicted before Mrs Thatcher came to power.

The houses are late-twentieth-century. They look different from the houses of previous ages; the requirements are different. What Terry's clients are looking for, he says, is 'a little, grand house'. That is, a house that proudly presents itself to the world as the residence of a gentleman, while remaining quite small, in country-house terms, and easy to run.[2] They have until recently been rather smaller than Kings Walden, with a span of eighteen or sixteen feet to the rooms, rather than twenty-one feet – although some of Terry's latest commissions have been almost on the Kings Walden scale. Whereas Kings Walden had a centrepiece of five bays and flanking wings, the Terry houses have so far been five bays across, and as a result the evolution of their façades can be seen as a developing theme (see Figures

1. 'To the Manor Reborn', *The Times*, 3 August 1983.
2. In Edwardian terms they are what would have been called 'the smaller country house'.

85, 95, 99). The houses tend not to have lodges or large wings of specialized service rooms. They never have dairies or the elaborate larders and ice rooms of earlier centuries. They do, on the other hand, quite often have a flat for the couple who look after the house, and a washing-machine room and drying room as well as the kitchen. There is unlikely to be a scullery. The kitchen may be big enough for the client and his family to eat in when they are by themselves, and correspondingly well fitted out. But the elevation of the kitchen into a room for the family is less universal than one might suppose: many of Terry's clients have cooks.

When it comes to the main rooms of the house, most clients like to have a dining room big enough to get twelve or fourteen comfortably round the table, and a formal drawing room to which they can go afterwards, as well as a less formal room for everyday family living. People still like to entertain. But, on the evidence of Terry's houses, they may not like their friends staying the night quite so much as before. That has become less convenient with fewer staff and possibly a more hectic pace of life, and three or four main bedrooms are often all that is asked for. If there are fewer bedrooms, however, there are more bathrooms, each bedroom being likely to have its own bathroom *en suite*. The bath and other bathroom fittings will be white: no Terry client has asked him for a coloured bath. Many people now like a bedroom floor that can be cut off and little heated during the week, and only opened up for returning children and friends at weekends.

The people for whom Terry builds are various. As an architect he naturally responds to the vigour, self-assurance and will to spend of the self-made entrepreneur – in eighteenth-century terms, the first rather than the fifth or sixth earl. Older families tend to be more cautious in their taste and preparedness to build. But of course this is by no means an invariable rule: Kings Walden Bury, for instance, was for the fourteenth baronet. With country houses, Terry believes that the art of architecture is not only to give the client what he wants, but to express his personality. This he does through the Classical language of architecture, as Summerson called it, and the use of Doric, Ionic and Corinthian orders. 'Everybody is one of the orders.' Some flamboyant clients cry out for Corinthian: Michael Heseltine and his wife both thought that this was the order for him (see Chapter 8). Others cannot bear things like finials. Working for a 'real old-fashioned aristocrat', as Terry described one client, he provided a 'plain house, with a good roof, big overhanging eaves, no gutters, no valleys – something that will last two hundred years'.

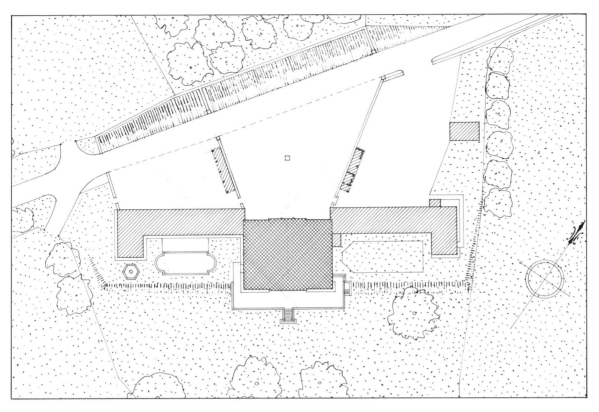

73. Waverton: site plan

WAVERTON HOUSE

A house of the latter kind is Waverton, near Moreton-in-Marsh in Gloucestershire, which was built in 1979 for the banker Jocelyn Hambro. He and his wife already had a house in Hampshire, but, owning a stud farm, they particularly wanted to build on the present site for the sake of the deep-rooted grass growing on the limestone, which helps strengthen the bones of horses, like grass in Ireland. As John Cornforth observed in *Country Life*,[3] Waverton has the feeling of being a stud house as much as a country house in the conventional sense. It has no grand approach. Rather, the drive is a lane that passes all the stud buildings before it reaches the house, and then gives into the forecourt from the side. But when it appears, the building seems a perfect miniature house: constructed of beautiful tawny Cotswold stone, and possessing all the dignity and some of the architecture

3. 6 August 1981.

74 and 75. Waverton: sash-window and pineapple

of a much larger building. Almost your first impression is that this house is extremely well built, and the sense of quality of finish is carried throughout the building. Other impressions are of simple, pleasing proportions, and of everything being as it should be. The façades are the embodiment of Terry's quest for order and harmony through Classicism.

The main lines of the house were settled quickly, within a week of the Hambros having come to Terry in early 1977. To either side of the central block are single-storey wings containing a staff flat and garages – although, because of the forecourt wall, the wings are not used to enhance the visual impact of the entrance façade. It almost seems a smaller house than it is. The entrance front has five bays, a pediment over the central three, pineapples at the angles of the pediment, a stone

86

roof with dormers, and an Ionic doorcase. But within this framework there are subtleties – in, for instance, the sizes of the windows, since the two on the ground floor immediately flanking the door are smaller than the windows in the end bays: they are the same size as those on the first floor. Since Waverton is a relatively small house, the adjustment was necessary for the doorcase not to be overpowered. The doorcase exemplifies Terry's love of simple numerical proportions, after Palladio: the order measures ten feet and the entablature two feet. Architrave, frieze and cornice are respectively eight inches, six inches and ten inches. The cornice is continued in the string course that wraps right round the building, which expresses the floor. On the south-facing garden façade – otherwise a mirror of the entrance front – is a three-bay loggia on the ground floor, the arches of which pick up the arched head to the front door.

Inside, the planning is simple and logical, showing Terry's preference for straightforward shapes and relationships, without surprises. In this 'little, grand house' the architectural effect is concentrated in the staircase hall, with its splendid Imperial stair rising up, branching, and returning above your head. There had been a similar stair in the Hambros' Hampshire house and Mrs Hambro had

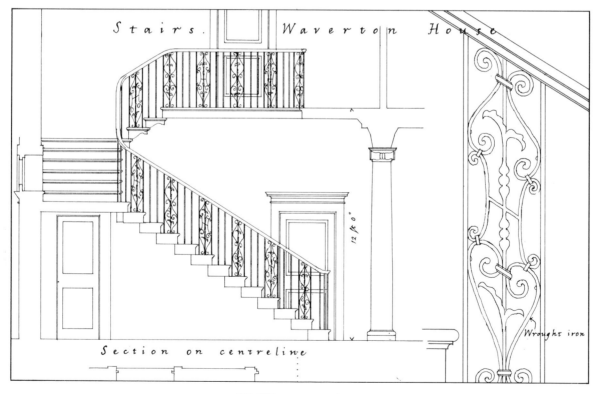

76. Waverton: staircase

87

particularly asked for one to be incorporated at Waverton. Terry therefore felt he should make this the dominant – some would call it the dominating – feature of the house. A grand, top-lit staircase in the centre of the house does, however, make sense, since it brings light into the building's heart, while the relatively dark areas around the outside of the stair are used for circulation. Behind the stair is the sun room, making use of the three arches of the loggia. It is overlooked – for borrowed light – by a lunette on the half landing of the stair, which is carried through from the lunette over the entrance door. Around the staircase hall are grouped the drawing room, dining room and study. The drawing room is twenty-seven feet nine inches by seventeen feet, which is not so large for a country house. For this room Terry designed the break-front cabinet for books and china that occupies the north wall.

It is the staircase hall that gives the interior its sense of generosity. The emphasis which it has been awarded also suggests that Waverton was built for a relatively formal way of life. Even so, it is an interesting reflection on late-twentieth-century

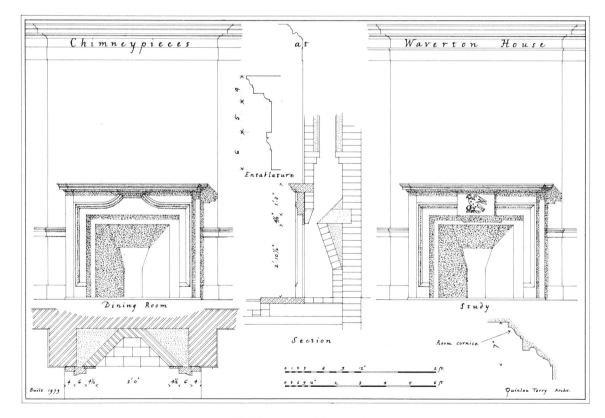

77. Waverton: chimneypieces

priorities that there is no back stair – a fact regretted by Mr Hambro's butler, Terence Rogers, who, before joining Mr Hambro, had served with his friend the late Lord Halifax at Garrowby for seventeen years.

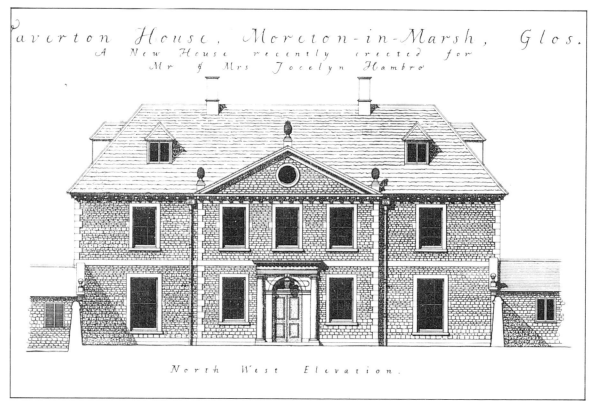

78. *Waverton: north elevation*

79. Waverton: north front

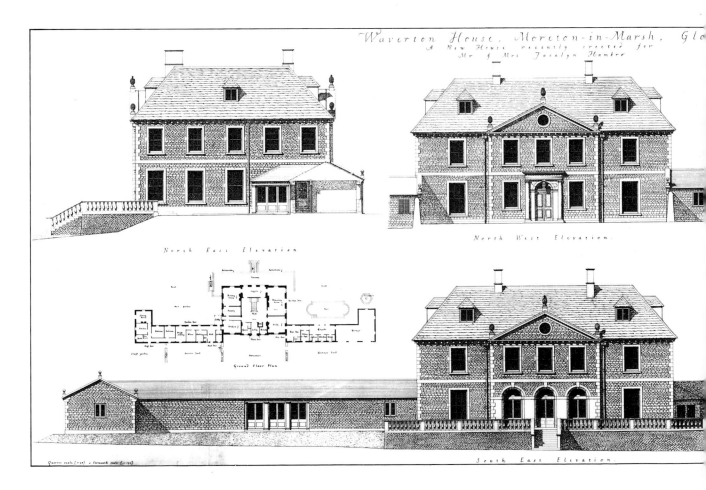

80. *Waverton: south front*

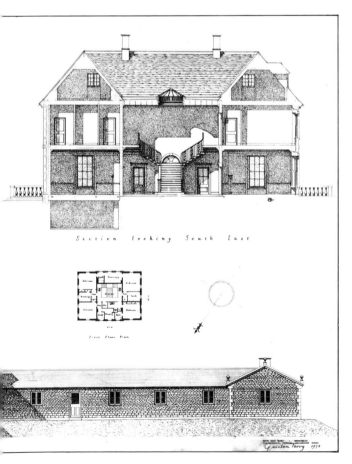

81. *Waverton: plans, elevations and section*

82. Waverton: front door

83. Waverton: staircase

84. Waverton: landing

QUINLAN TERRY

Building houses is a very personal form of architecture, and the more strongly the client expresses his or her hopes and desires, the more interesting the result is likely to be. For the challenge of incorporating the particular demands of a particular client into the Classical framework immediately kills any chance that the design might be derivative. It forces the architect to be inventive. One of Terry's most fascinating houses, from the point of view both of the architecture and of what it says about the requirements of late-twentieth-century life, is Newfield House in Yorkshire. The client, Michael Abrahams, who has a carpet manufacturing business in Bradford, Leeds and London, thought about the design very hard indeed.

Newfield lies to the west of Ripon, on the edge of the moors. Mr Abrahams was born and brought up in the area, and he and his wife had a rambling Victorian house a dozen or so miles away. At the time of building Mr Abrahams was already Master of the West of Yore Hunt. There are about a hundred and thirty acres, used either as paddocks or for grazing sheep. Originally a farmhouse lay a little lower down the hill from the site on which it was decided to build. The advantage of the new site is that it stands up proud with views in all directions over the well-hedged, rolling country. So the house announces itself splendidly from the little road that runs across the end of the drive. The disadvantage is that, until the new planting has grown up, it will lose the shelter which the farmhouse had enjoyed. Newfield is the little, grand house *par excellence* – 'unique', says the owner, in appearing 'to get smaller as you approach'.

The original idea had been to have something like Kings Walden Bury. Therefore in November 1978 Terry submitted a design very similar in feeling to that house, with, on both main fronts, wide and plain end bays contrasting with a rich colonnaded five-bay centrepiece – varied with rustication on the lower floor on the south. It would have been somewhat smaller than Kings Walden, with a big cross hall with a curving stair giving off it, and a drawing room and dining room to either side. Long wings would have come forward forming an entrance forecourt on the north. There was a family area formed by dining room, kitchen and a sitting room round the kitchen. Architect and client were still feeling their way.

In the course of the winter, however, the Abrahams stayed with a relation in Twickenham and saw Marble Hill. Mr Abrahams at once recognized that this should be the model. So by February 1979 a new design showing a main block

94

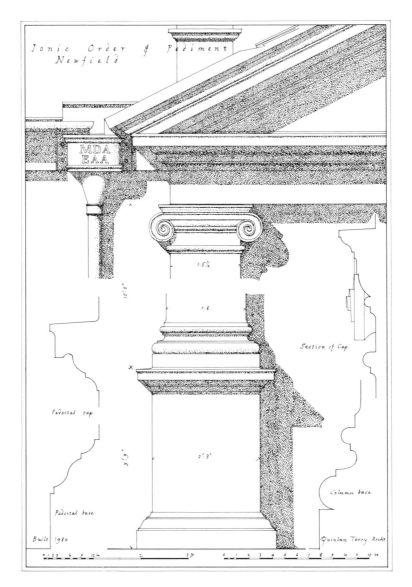

85. Newfield: Ionic order and pediment

about the size of Marble Hill, with a pediment but without a basement, was prepared. The influence has been maintained throughout the design, for instance in the fireplaces of the drawing room and hall, derived from, respectively, those in the hall and dining parlour at Marble Hill. But the new house still had big flanking wings. Then, that spring, the Abrahams went to the Veneto to look at the villas. What most struck them was one of the things that, earlier, had most struck Erith:

95

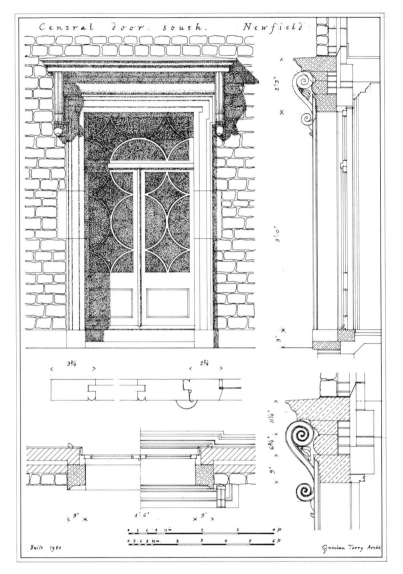

86. Newfield: central door, south front

the way in which this architecture was genuinely rural, with the farm buildings forming an integral part of the house, often enhancing its effect by acting as detached flanking blocks. This suggested flankers at Newfield. They take the form of a stable and a hay barn, both weatherboarded, on either side of a big sweep of gravel drive. They appear on the designs by August 1979, and Terry and the Abrahams knew they had found the solution.

To describe the house it is best to start with the plan. The Abrahams' old Victorian house had put them off unnecessary space which had to be heated and

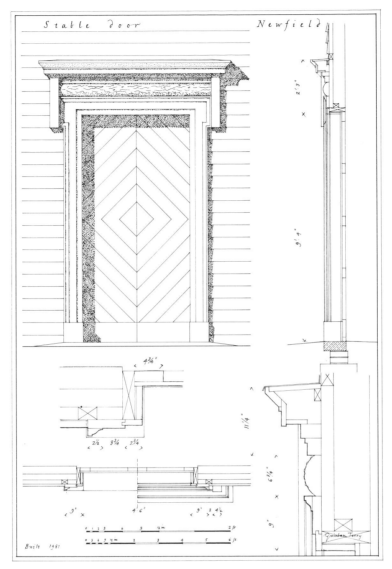

87. Newfield: stable door

cleaned; moreover, Mrs Abrahams does not like domestic staff permanently in the house, and she prefers to do her own cooking. This argued for a house of manageable proportions, with the kitchen combined with a family living room, so that Mrs Abrahams did not feel banished before every meal. You enter the house from the north into a vestibule, decorated with masonry jointing in *trompe-l'œil*. This gives into the hall, which has a stone floor. In the centre stands a dining table made by a friend of the owner and painted with birds in imitation of pietra dura. Windows on the south side of the room look out over what will be terraced

97

gardens and a ha-ha. Opposite them is the small dog-leg staircase, and doors to lavatory and drinks room. The hall is in the centre of the house. To the east is the drawing room – well proportioned but not big – with Mr Abrahams' study beyond. The latter has three French windows on the south, a door and a window on the west, and an internal window giving extra light to the drawing room on the east. Along the north wall is a bookcase with triangular and segmental pediments, designed by Terry. To the west of the hall comes the big lived-in kitchen-living room (called by Mr Abrahams 'Coronation Street'), and balancing the study, a sun room for use in the summer. There is no dining room: when there is a party, they eat in the hall. It is an arrangement which the Abrahams find works very well. Upstairs are four family bedrooms and a guest suite. One-storey wings in brick come forward to either side of the forecourt, containing utility rooms and flats for Mr Abrahams' groom and farm manager. In the most approved Victorian manner, the windows from these flats look only away from the house, preserving the privacy of all concerned.

Outside, Newfield is approached axially along a double lime avenue the full width of the house. Seen from the end of this avenue you think that, with the flankers, it is a very big house. When you get into the courtyard you realize that it is quite small – very small by Georgian, Victorian or Edwardian standards. The flankers therefore have the opposite effect from the self-deprecating wings at Waverton. But at Newfield you also have the feeling of entering a self-enclosed, well-ordered rural world, with perhaps someone chopping wood or shifting hay in the barn, or taking a hunter out of the stable. (The barn contains a year's supply of hay for the stable: there is a smaller barn behind the stable to hold enough for weekly supplies.)

As at Waverton, the five-bay entrance front has a one-three-one rhythm, with the centre three bays pedimented and slightly projecting. The pediment has a cartouche rather than an *œil-de-bœuf*: there are no dormers. But the façade also has a 'giant' Ionic order. Though the order is giant in the sense of going through two storeys, it is in fact still relatively small, so the cornice to this has no modillions – an idea of the client's which at first shocked Terry but could be justified by reference to Palladio. From the first an important consideration in the design was that it should be in keeping with the country around, and this had been one of the factors militating against a Modern design. Therefore, in choosing the materials for the house Terry and his client looked carefully at the architecture of the locality, which the latter knew from boyhood. It is an area in which brick and stone – in particular, cobbles – are used together, not infrequently in the same

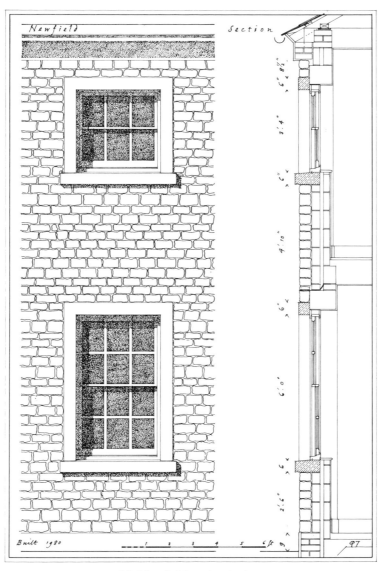

88. Newfield: sash-windows

building. The bricks originally came from the Bromborough clay fields. So you find brick buildings with stone relieving arches to the windows, and cobble buildings which have arches of brick. A house such as nearby Sleningford Hall has a stone centre block and brick wings, with cobble estate walls. North Stainley Hall is brick with a cut cobble stable block. For Newfield it was decided to use cut cobble as the principal material for the main block, brick and pantiles for the wings, and rough cobble for the ancillary buildings and walls. The Ionic order is stone and so are the quoins; the big Venetian finials are in reconstituted stone.

99

Otherwise, however, the centrepiece of the entrance front is stucco: not a happy material in so exposed a location, although it will not suffer so much from the weather when the trees have grown up. The south front, which looks out superbly over the landscape, is simpler, with no order. There is a pediment over the central three bays, and a doorcase with brackets. The lead hoppers to the rainwater pipes bear monograms of Mr Abrahams' children's initials.

With its farm, stables and wings, Newfield looks from a distance less like one relatively small house (not much bigger in floor area, as the owner points out, than a speculative house) than a small village, and that is precisely the sense of 'country Palladian', as Erith would have put it, that the owner hoped to achieve.

With the essay 'Genuine Classicism' (see Chapter 11), Newfield was submitted to the Philippe Rotthier Foundation's European Award Scheme for the Reconstruction of the City and won Terry the £5,000 prize. Moreover, it delights the owner that the house is still the subject of strongly argued views in North Yorkshire – between those who say it is too small and those who say it is just right.

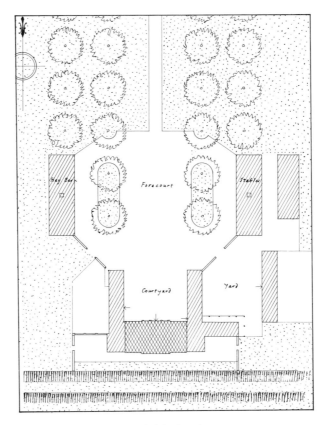

89. Newfield: site plan

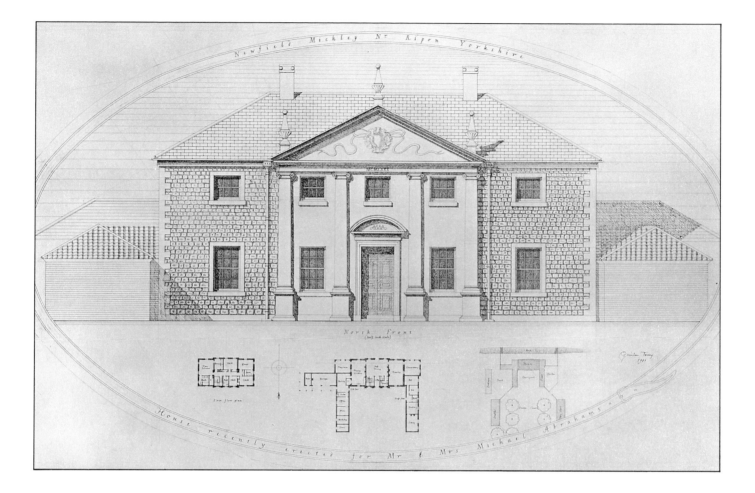

90. Newfield: elevation and plans

101

91. Newfield: north front

92. Newfield: barn

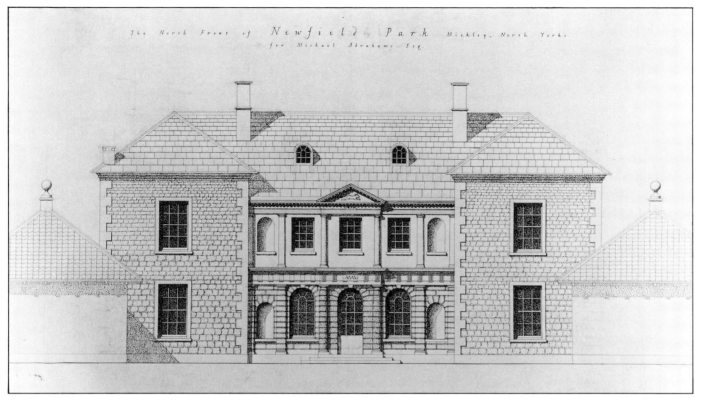

The North Front of Newfield Park Mickley, North Yorks.
for Michael Abrahams Esq.

93. *Newfield: north front, first scheme*

94. *Newfield: stable*

95. Newfield: door, north front   *96. Newfield: chimneypiece*

97. Newfield: door, south front   98. Newfield: chimneypiece

QUINLAN TERRY

TWO UNBUILT DESIGNS

A client who – had things worked out differently – might have proved one of the
most stimulating of Terry's career was Keith Hunt, head of the meteoric Exchange
Securities and Commodities Ltd of Warwick. In October 1982 his personal
assistant wrote to Terry saying that Mr Hunt had just bought Hampton Lucy
House near Warwick, a seventeenth- and eighteenth-century five-bay house, with
views over the Avon and to the park at Charlecote. Major internal works were
required. And as the letter continued: 'The thought is also that the entrance
forecourt is made more imposing and that a large winter garden be added and that
the gardens, which at the moment are very non-descript, be in part formalized
with an architectural garden perhaps with trellis work or a temple of some
description or a water garden be created.' By November Terry was ready to send
Mr Hunt a first design, showing a long gallery added to the south front, with a
saloon and dining room forming pavilions. The centre three bays of the long
gallery would have had an attached Doric order on a Borromini-esque curve. But
it was not hot enough for Mr Hunt. 'Overall, you are being far too conservative,
tentative and economical,' he wrote on 4 January 1983. 'What is required is
grandeur on a small scale: the gardens can then take their cue from this façade.'
His idea was to have a stunner of a façade on the south, which would bowl his
guests over as they walked round from the restrained entrance court. 'The essential
qualities that it must possess are drama, power, vigour,' he wrote. ' ... Con-
venience is secondary to the architectural qualities of the façade: these qualities
must be paramount.' From the tone of the letter Mr Hunt could have become a
very exciting client indeed. 'As to style for the South façade, whatever is produced
must be undoubtedly late-C.20 classical,' he continued enthusiastically. 'It must
not be a copy or imitation ... I want the best work you have yet done, and
hopefully, are ever capable of doing ... ' Possessing an impressive knowledge of
architectural history, he suggested that Palladio's early schemes for the Villa
Sarego might serve as the theme.

Such commissions, and such clients, are rare, so Terry entered into the spirit of
the game. On 25 January 1983, he sketched a new south elevation, bursting with
vitality. A giant rusticated order was to stride across the façade, with two-storey
arches in the end and centre bays and aedicules in those to either side of the centre.
There was a pediment, and the parapet had a flamboyant alternation of obelisks
and finials. To either side were pavilions with Venetian windows. Three days later
the sketch had been drawn out: volutes now eased the transition between centre

block and wings. Explaining the design, Terry wrote:

I feel that a giant order is called for and I found to my satisfaction that the existing cornice on the north front is almost exactly right to take a correctly sized frieze, architrave and column underneath it. This therefore argues that Francis Smith of Warwick [thought to have been involved at Hampton Lucy] implied a giant order in the rustications on the corners of the house on the north side. A bold treatment on the south is therefore logical.

Applications for listed building consent and planning approval were made in the early spring.

But, alas, this most promising of projects got no further. Exchange Securities collapsed – and Mr Hunt disappeared, owing several million pounds to the Inland Revenue and a smaller figure to Quinlan Terry. However, this had the one merit of preventing what might have been a clash with Georgian purists, who might have felt obliged to defend this modest eighteenth-century house from late-twentieth-century ebullience, however appealing.

Another unexecuted design is that for the belvedere at Henbury Hall, Maccles-field, for Sebastian de Ferranti. From the first it was intended as the realization of the owner's strong ideas derived from Palladio's Villa Capra or Rotonda near Vicenza, which were rendered in a series of paintings by Felix Kelly. Terry's design, however, was not sufficiently close to this vision to satisfy Mr de Ferranti and he withdrew in favour of Julian Bicknell; with the latter as architect the house has now been completed. The Rotonda was adapted to several English houses in the eighteenth century, notably Chiswick, Mereworth, Foots Cray and Nuttall, and surprisingly perhaps, Terry found that the Rotonda theme was perfectly suited to modern needs. 'You get a raised basement floor, which is practical – kitchen, utilities, dining room, safes, gun room and everything else. You can protect that very well. Above that you have a ground floor which is just parade, then a top floor which is quite economical for bedrooms. For modern living it is not totally ridiculous.'[4] But Mrs de Ferranti, with the experience of running a house, points out that lifts are necessary, especially between the kitchen and dining room.

4. *Times*, ibid. The new design by Julian Bicknell is described in John Martin Robinson, *The Latest Country Houses*, 1984.

99. Farnborough Downs: elevation and plans

MERKS HALL AND FARNBOROUGH DOWNS

Merks Hall and Farnborough Downs are variations on the same theme, the one expansive and dominating, the other almost as small as a grand idea can be. They show a satisfying sense of development in Terry's style, for each resolves certain problems in the earlier houses. Merks in particular demonstrates how Classicism, once down on its knees, is now back on top, since the house replaces another built in only 1961 in what Terry describes as the 'Health Centre Style' – plate glass windows, concrete tiles, no symmetry. The owner, Mr Richard Wallis, having bought the house for the sake of the established grounds, had already lived there for nineteen years, during which time he tried several times to change and modify the house, but saw no hope of improving it. When he asked Terry what he thought, the latter replied: 'It's not a gentleman's house.' This sealed its fate; it had to come down. But the 1961 house had in turn usurped the place of a Georgian house. As the walls of the present building rise triumphantly on their ridge above Great Dunmow in Essex – and Merks, with its belvedere, will be visible for miles around – there is a feeling in more than one way that the old order has been restored.

Mr Wallis went to Terry after having seen Waverton in *Country Life*, and said that he wanted a house just like it. It is now only when one looks at the plan, however, that one realizes that the kinship is so close. For, like Waverton, Merks is arranged symmetrically around a big central staircase hall, with an Imperial stair – though the stair here has benefited from the increased scale of the building as a whole: appropriately there is a greater expansiveness than at Waverton. From the

100 and 101. Farnborough Downs: frontispiece and finials

outside the two houses look like distant cousins rather than mother and daughter. Translating Waverton from Gloucestershire to Essex called for basic modifications: most obviously Merks is brick and slate rather than stone and stone tile. Then the requirements of the Wallises came into it. They did not need a staff flat in the house and were prepared to have the washing machine, wine store and other utilities in the basement. This did away with the two one-storey wings of Waverton, making a more compact design. Finally the design grew. It was conceived from the start as a bigger house than Waverton, with a span of eighteen feet and a proportionate room height of fourteen feet from floor to floor. The plan is deeper, and with its basement Merks was also destined to be tall. When it came to the roof, however, Terry played on this even further, giving it dormers and a crowning cupola – immediately directing the imagination to the 1670s rather than the 1810s. Merks commands the landscape, formed by the park of the original Georgian house, with a truly aristocratic self-confidence. Or as Terry puts it: 'When you see it, you think this is where big men have been.'

Because it is to be seen from a distance, the south front is plain and bold. Decoration is concentrated on the entrance front on the north, fully revealed only when you enter the octagonal courtyard. Waverton's Ionic, though it controlled the design, only flanked the front door. But at Merks the centrepiece has superimposed orders in the manner of Kings Walden Bury. The upper order, which is Ionic, is three-quarters the height of the lower Doric: a proportion which Palladio liked. And the cornice of the upper order is very big so that it can serve as the cornice to the whole house.

While the windows on the main fronts of Kings Walden Bury were evenly spaced, the central window of the Merks centrepiece is larger than those on either side. This had implications for the other elements of the Classical grid. Stretching the cornice, for instance, meant that it was not possible to have a modillion centrally over the two inner columns – an unavoidable solecism. It also prevented an even spacing of triglyphs in the Doric frieze. 'When Italian architects got in trouble, I find that they changed the subject,' says Terry. Here he 'changed the subject' by placing a monogrammed tablet over the entrance door, suavely distracting one's attention from the increased width of metope. The columns and finials are in natural Portland stone; so too are the floor of the entrance hall and the staircase inside.

Terry likes the noble effect of few, big windows as opposed to a larger number of smaller ones. The windows at Waverton were four foot by eight and those of Newfield three foot six by seven (smaller because the house is in the north); but at

Merks they are four foot six by nine on the ground floor of the entrance front. In a favourite mannerism, the windows of the first floor have been made slightly smaller – three foot nine by seven foot six. On the south front the ground-floor windows go down to the floor, so that it is possible to walk out through them onto the terrace: the upper sash pushes up into the lintel. A particular success at Merks has been the east front, where there is a Palladian window to one of the son's bedrooms on the first floor. Unlike Kings Walden Bury with its awkward spacing of windows on the side elevation, Merks has three show fronts, not just two.

The quality of the interior of Merks can best be judged from the section (Figure 102). The plan is a double square, with the staircase in the centre. This is top-lit from the dome which supports the lantern, the top of which is seventy foot above the ground level. The geometry of Merks works better than that of Waverton, where it was not possible to put the lantern centrally over the stair. Although at the time of writing the house has yet to be roofed, let alone decorated, one can already see that the rooms will be almost Kentian in the strength of their architectural character. The drawing-room doorcases have broken pediments with volutes, and in the drawing-room and dining-room fireplaces Terry has at last been able to realize his long pent-up urge to design a serpentine front.

While Merks stands up proud on a rise, the setting for Farnborough Downs could not be more different. Though it has particularly good views across the Berkshire Downs to the south, it is so well sheltered on the east side by a hill that you do not see it until you have almost arrived. The scale and character of the house also make it the perfect complement to Merks.

For many years Mr Adrian and the Hon. Mrs White had used the old farmhouse on the site as a country cottage, but with a view to living there more permanently they felt they needed more space. Their natural taste is for the Regency and they therefore needed rooms with tall ceilings. But partly for reasons of planning permission, it was decided not to build from new but to retain the existing structure. Terry's solution was to build a new wing that would become, clearly, the main block, while not dwarfing the old. It has succeeded so well that visitors to the house often mistake the new wing for the original.

Because of the relationship with the old work, the new wing has a miniaturist quality which is made the most of. The surroundings are not those of a great formal house. Farnborough Downs is approached by a country lane and it is first seen on the diagonal, as you go down from the brow of the hill. Further, with the entrance front facing south, the lawn in front of the house inevitably became somewhere to sit out; and in the small link wing joining the new block to the old is a trelliswork arcade for that purpose. There is a mood of intimacy about the house, of Classical dignity married to domesticity, and it does not seem inappropriate that a three-sided bay – essentially Victorian in concept – breaks out on the east elevation.

Deliberately, the centrepiece was made as flamboyant as the small scale would permit. The object was the reverse of Newfield: not breadth but delicacy. As at Merks there is a superimposed order with what is now an almost diminutive pediment, which Terry says he had always wanted to do. The façade is three bays wide, and there are three dormers, with alternating segmental and triangular pediments, in the very deep roof. Although the client preferred thin glazing bars, again the roof and dormers give a seventeenth-century feeling, but for very practical reasons: the extra bedrooms in the attic can be shut off and unheated when not being used by guests. The development of the attic in this way is becoming a characteristic feature of Terry's houses. Also, at Farnborough Downs a tall house was needed to capitalize on the views. A great disadvantage of the old house had been that, despite an attractive situation, it had not been possible to enjoy the views from inside, since the windows faced not down the valley but into the hill. Attic rooms also allow some dramatic effects: the uppermost finial has been consciously placed in front of the middle dormer, which lights a bathroom, so that it can act as a piece of sculpture, seen unexpectedly close, when you look out.

As for the accommodation, the new wing is a very grand version of a two-up, two-down. On the ground floor the dining room and the drawing room stand to either side of the central staircase hall. The dining room was designed to seat fourteen, and has one splendidly big window looking north (in an evening room this is not a drawback). As a party of fourteen will need more room in the drawing room after dinner than they do round the dining-room table, the bay was introduced. As well as filling the room with light and making the most of the views over the Downs, it provides a greater feeling of space than the room would otherwise have had.

102. Merks Hall

103. Farnborough Downs: trellised porch

104. Farnborough Downs: south front

105. Farnborough Downs: frontispiece (facing)

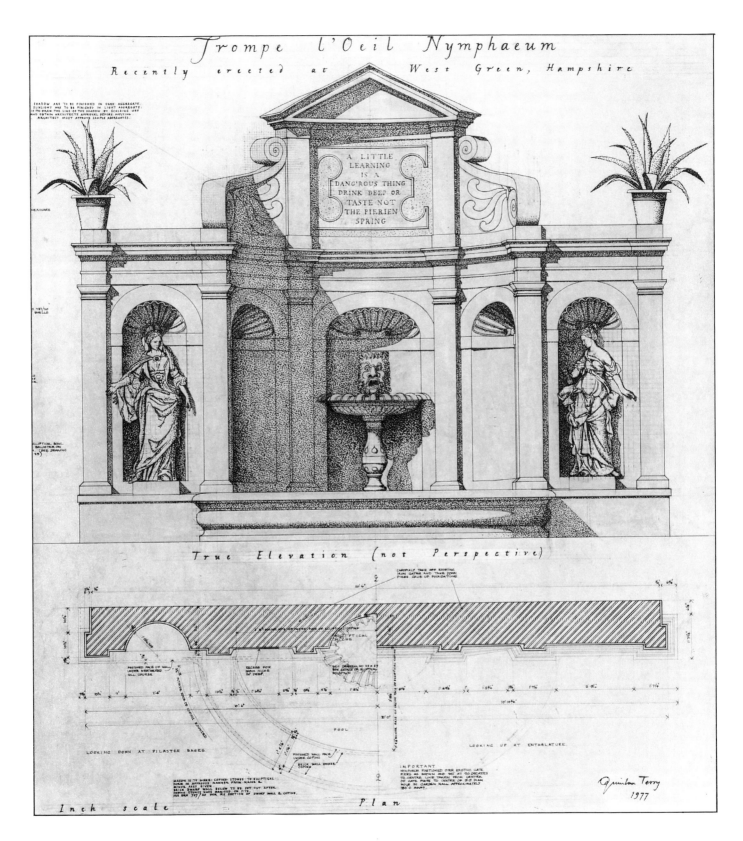

Trompe l'Oeil Nymphaeum
Recently erected at West Green, Hampshire

A LITTLE
LEARNING
IS A
DANG'ROUS THING
DRINK DEEP OR
TASTE NOT
THE PIERIEN
SPRING

True Elevation (not Perspective)

Inch scale *Plan*

Quinlan Terry
1977

106. West Green: Nymphaeum, 1977

CHAPTER EIGHT

GARDEN BUILDINGS, STABLES AND *TROMPE-L'ŒIL*

Terry's own house is Higham Hall, in a scattered hamlet about a mile away from his Dedham office. It is a four-square gentleman's house of white Suffolk brick, built in about 1810 – slightly Soanic and austere. It is big enough for a family of five children, Elizabeth, Anna, Francis (the one boy, who has, incidentally, thoughts of following his father into architecture), Martha and Sophia. It is also next to the church, although not the one that the Terrys attend because it holds a service only once a month; and at the end of the drive is a big barn full of a neighbouring farmer's cows, which Terry finds a soothing subject for contemplation when puzzling out an architectural idea in his head. At one time it seemed likely that Terry would spend much of his practice working for local landowners, altering their houses, so he blends naturally into the country life of this prosperous corner of Suffolk – quite literally, when he dons the uniform of green wellies, Barbour and cap for the Higham point to point.

But, though it might look so from the outside, one would not say that Higham Hall was typical of the squire's houses of the area. The family has been there five years, and already their taste – it is not just Terry's – has been stamped on it. Inside this is architectural rather than homely: *trompe-l'œil* stone-blocking and mahogany-graining in the hall, a bravura piece of false perspective in the library, Greek Doric columns and frieze round the big kitchen where they eat *en famille*, which several members of the family helped paint. *Trompe-l'œil* and false perspective are enthusiasms which Terry culled from Rome. His first experience of false perspective had been at the Palazzo Barberini, and he later found that, once your eye is in for visual tricks, they are to be seen 'almost everywhere'.

While at the British School at Rome he encouraged Jeremy Blake to undertake a study of the subject, which was later published as *La Falsa Prospettiva*, and Blake

117

is now in Terry's office. But it was not, interestingly, until after Erith's death that he began to practise such skills himself – for instance, in his and his wife's bedroom in their old house, Winterfloods. This extraordinary room, where the floor raked so steeply that it seemed the furniture would roll away, was decorated with niches containing Old Testament figures, nearly life-size, in grisaille. Alas for 'trompe', the next owner of the house had the scheme painted out and it is perpetuated only in photographs.

If Terry's values seem to some people escapist and other-worldly, life at Higham is their vindication. Being a Classicist does not mean that Terry lives in the past; but he has worked out a *modus vivendi* with the present which preserves some of the most agreeable qualities of old-fashioned country life. The landscape in which the house is set is important to the sense of unspoilt rural peace. Higham Hall is surrounded by watermeadows, since the big, grassy garden contains the point where the river Brett (the family like to call it the Brenta) joins the Stour. Immediately around the house, as you would expect of a Classicist, the setting is formal. Two years ago earth-moving equipment was brought in to create a terrace, and Terry has grandly planted an avenue down to the Stour aligned on Langham Hall, standing on a hill on the horizon. Well, not in fact as grandly as it would first appear. The distance to the river is far too short for a normal avenue, so the trees are holly. And they have been planted in sharp false perspective to increase the sense of length. It is so unexpected that it works. At the end of the avenue Terry has built a boat house of six by six oak timbers and a pantiled roof for the family punt.

It will be clear from the surroundings in which Terry lives his own life at home that *trompe-l'œil*, false perspective and garden buildings are an important subject to

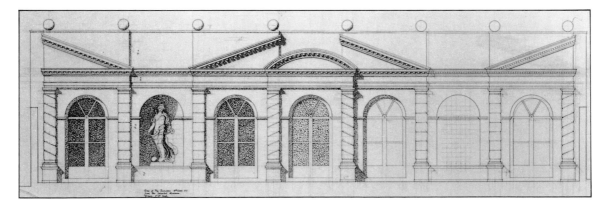

107. Little Roydon House: screen wall, 1978

118

him. Garden buildings sometimes give opportunities for *trompe-l'œil* and false perspective that more sober commissions do not. This is the virtue of follies from the architect's point of view: they are little pieces of pure architecture. A surprising percentage of Terry's professional life has been spent designing them.

WEST GREEN HOUSE

This quality of being 'pure architecture' dispels the paradox that otherwise might seem to exist in Terry's enthusiasm for follies. For designing follies does not conflict with his fundamental seriousness. Indeed, the effort of mind that goes into the designing of even incidental garden ornaments can be intense. Terry has been particularly fortunate that, in the Hon. Alistair McAlpine (now Lord McAlpine of West Green), he has had a client of sufficient flamboyance to enter into folly building with the gusto – and the seriousness – it deserves. He was fortunate, too, that in the mid-1970s, when Lord McAlpine employed him most intensively, he had the time to give of his best to the work.

Lord McAlpine gave Terry some of the few commissions to be realized in the period immediately following Erith's death, when the Baha'i temple was being designed. If the development of his garden at West Green House in Hampshire is continued – and Lord McAlpine says that it will be – it will deserve a high place in the history of the 'philosophical' garden, certainly for the wit of the details if not for the consistency with which the overall scheme has been conceived. Sadly a fire in 1982 severely damaged the house itself, leading Lord McAlpine to spend his unstoppable energies elsewhere while restoration was in progress. To the National Trust, which owns West Green House (Lord McAlpine is their tenant there),

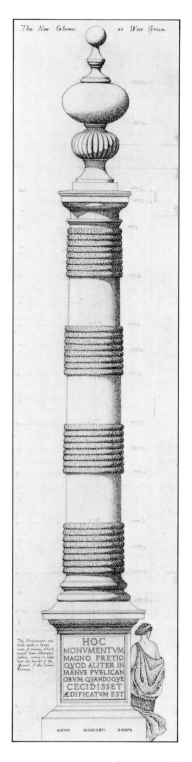

108. West Green: column, 1976

119

109 and 110. West Green: elliptical urn, 1980, and triumphal arch, to the first lady Prime Minister, 1979

this hiatus in the garden work may not have been wholly unwelcome. Ironically both West Green and West Wycombe in Buckinghamshire, the two gardens which Terry has most adorned with follies, belong to the National Trust. For both houses are basically eighteenth-century and the building of Classical follies is, one would have thought, very much in the spirit of their Georgian and Regency owners. But the new follies are causing some head scratching on the part of the

120

Trust. They might – they *will* – in time become part of the historic character of the house. At some point the Trust will become obliged to restore them. As the fire damage at West Green has now been fully repaired (Terry was architect),[1] the Trust may soon have cause to ponder this dilemma afresh.

At West Green, the first of the follies announces itself before you turn down the present drive to the house. For a great column and finial of Portland stone have been placed near the road, at the end of a new lime avenue on axis with the entrance front of the house. A new drive along this avenue is being formed. But the placing of the column so near the public road could with justice be called provocative. The column, however handsome, is quite deliberately and flagrantly useless, and makes no concessions on this point to mealy-mouthed notions of economy, modesty and reserve. It was conceived at the time when the Labour government was threatening to bring in a wealth tax. Lord McAlpine, who belongs to the McAlpine construction family and is Treasurer of the Conservative Party, expressed his feelings in architecture, Terry devising the legend: '*Hoc monumentum magno pretio quod aliter in manus publicanorum quandoque cecidisset aedificatum est*' ('This monument was built with a large sum of money, which would have otherwise fallen, sooner or later, into the hands of the tax-gatherers'). Terry's first design, dated July 1975, shows a column with rubble rustication and a Portland stone finial, surrounded by a thatched hut at the base. It is similar to Erith and Terry's croquet pavilion at Aynho. By November 1975 he was proposing a straight column with vermiculated bands and a flaming urn. This developed into what we see now: a column with bands of rustication which are themselves banded, like the Michelin Man's tyres, and with a bold and bulbous finial on top. Alas, the triumphal arch with obelisks which Lord McAlpine proposed erecting in honour of the first lady prime minister of Great Britain in 1979 was designed but never built.

Lord McAlpine first met Terry the day after Erith's death. But his tastes are not only for the Classical. Before coming to Terry he had built up the notable collection of fifty-nine modern sculptures which he generously gave to the Tate Gallery in 1970. When you arrive at West Green today, the front door is still guarded by a skinny horsewoman in bronze by David Wynne – the attenuated proportions making an unexpected contrast to Terry's Classical gates. One might have thought that this marked a progression of taste, but no. Lord McAlpine, who is also a collector of prehistoric and primitive material, sees all his different

---

1. The restored and redecorated house was described in *The World of Interiors*, April 1985.

interests as interlocking. He is still buying the work of avant-garde artists like Kenneth Noland and Morris Louis, and he does not believe this to be in any way incompatible with his enthusiasm for Terry – because Terry is not a pasticheur. He stands, says Lord McAlpine somewhat puzzlingly, 'absolutely in the tradition of Rothko and Pollock'. More understandable is the relationship between Lord McAlpine's liking for primitive artefacts and his garden at West Green. For the lawns across which the follies – so carefully contrived – are seen have not been rolled velvet smooth, and the flowerbeds have not been planted out with begonias in rows. On the contrary, the grass in some areas is not cut and the weeds seem to do as well as the plants. As Lord McAlpine explains, the idea is of a formal garden in a state of decay with nature on the point of reasserting herself – an approach which perhaps, without anyone realizing it, echoes the wilderness gardens of the eighteenth century, with their uprooted tree trunks and Salvator Rosa effects.

The house itself is a perfect red-brick dream: Gibbsian, with sympathetic pre-First World War additions. It is entered by a forecourt on the north, and the gardens open up to the east and south. If you take the gate in the right-hand wall of the forecourt you find yourself at the end of a series of terraced lawns that run due east from the house. This, and the big walled vegetable garden to the left, represent the formal part of the garden. Here Terry's work is first seen in two urns

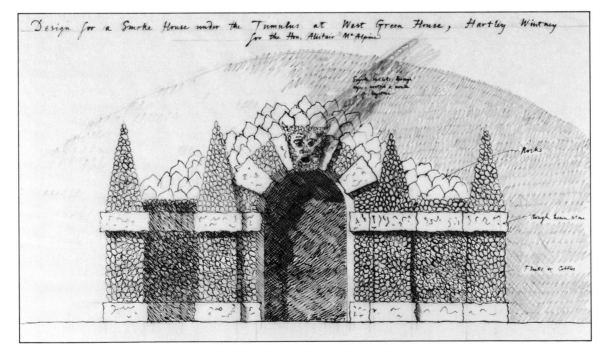

111. West Green: Smoke House, 1981

on the second level of lawn. These urns may not strike you as more than beautiful ornaments: the sort of thing you can buy at Crowther's, except modern rather than eighteenth-century. But the important point is that they *are* modern: in other words, that the skills of designing and making them have been perpetuated; and that they are very, very difficult to do. They illustrate the seriousness of garden architecture. The urns are oval and gadrooned (bulging in shape), and also fluted in spirals. To keep the flutes parallel around the ellipsoid was a deep mathematical puzzle. The design took Terry a whole month to detail and the mason three months to make. It does not seem obviously in the tradition of Jackson Pollock; but elsewhere there is room in the Classical tradition for Lord McAlpine's taste for the primitive to be given expression in the garden, for a rustic hut has been proposed for the top of the Tumulus which lies to the left of the long lawn.

The Tumulus has yet to be finished. It is a mound created out of compost and garden rubbish, and will therefore require a certain amount of time to reach its full size. The hut is to be a homage to the French rationalist Laugier, who maintained that all Classical architecture had developed from, and could be explained in terms of, the primitive dwellings made by man's remotest ancestors. The drawing, dated 14 July 1980, notes: 'Structure of Ash poles lashed together with rope in the manner used by our ancestors when they came out of the forests to construct shelters from the elements …' Although this design has yet to be executed, a Doric hut representing a similar idea has already been constructed at West Green, and Terry's fascination with Laugier can also be seen in the West Wycombe cricket pavilion (Figure 138).

A scheme to turn the Tumulus itself into a Smoke House for smoking meat and fish was drawn in March 1981, and Lord McAlpine still proposes to carry it out. The Smoke House will have a heavily rusticated entrance with pyramids and a great circular mask (already carved) above the door. Smoke will pour out of the mask's eyes and mouth, which are hollow, when the Smoke House is being used. However, while it is waiting to fulfil its ultimate function, the Tumulus already has a purpose as a viewpoint for the rest of the garden. Sight lines are shown streaming from it in all directions on the plan. Three plunge into the informal southern part of the garden. One reveals the Chinese Bridge to the island on the lake; another the bird cage on the island; the third the Doric Lodge in the southern corner – again with tree-trunk columns and block capitals to illustrate the origins of the Doric order. A grotto has been proposed for the south-east wall. (Erith and Terry had experience of designing a grotto in 1972, the client being Victor Lownes of the Playboy Club: it was to be for his country house at Stocks

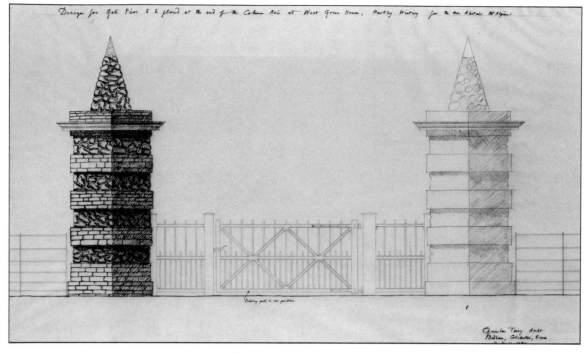

112. West Green: gates, 1983

in Hertfordshire, and would have comprised an inner pool in a vaulted octagon with niches, a big outer pool, and a sauna. It is not very surprising that neither the architects nor the client felt wholly compatible with each other, and the design remained just a design.)

From the Tumulus you can also see the most remarkable of all the follies at West Green, the Nymphaeum or 'Prospettiva' – but it is better to approach this through the vegetable garden. For in the centre of the west wall is a circular opening known as the Moon Gate that is the intended viewing point. The Nymphaeum is – well, does one say what it is or what it is not? In outline it is a little decorative building with a raised central section, with pediment and volutes, and wings. So far so good. The whole centrepiece curves inwards, and in the wings there are shell-headed niches with statues. No. That is how it appears; but it is not so, because this is a dazzling piece of *trompe-l'œil* in stone and paint. The eye deceives the mind – but, extraordinarily enough, the mind must be a willing victim, as there is no attempt at a wholly naturalistic illusion. True, when you get close, you see that – as a refinement of cunning – shadows are painted both on flat surfaces and those which are genuinely three-dimensional (the statues and the projecting basin of the fountain in the centre). But the shadows are a uniform

124

mid-chocolate colour. This is not the real colour of shadows on a yellowish stone. Yet there is no doubt: you *are* taken in. Having studied the subject in Italy Terry believes that, to enjoy a false perspective fully, it is important for the viewer to know that he is being tricked. If he is simply deceived without being alerted to what is going on, there is no pleasure in it. Hence the slight exaggeration. According to the drawing of February 1976, the original thought had been to have the light and shadow shown by light and dark coloured pebbles pushed into the stucco – a more durable solution than paint. In form, the Nymphaeum is modelled quite closely on the fountain of Santa Maria della Scala in the Via Garibaldi, in Rome, which Terry had measured nine years earlier (Figure 23). But at West Green, the *trompe-l'œil* also serves a practical, country purpose: it hides a cow shed for the fields at the back. It is intended that the fountain should be activated by the changes in level of the water in a trough at the back, caused by cows drinking.

While much has been built at West Green, so many ideas have been thrown up in the air that it would be unrealistic to expect all of them to have been caught. Among the dropped ones are a Chinese orangery, a pagoda boathouse and a 'Trellis Gate leading to the Chambers Ornamental Garden'. Lord McAlpine's enthusiasm for Chambers dates from 1975, when he proposed rescuing Cham-

113. Salute birdcage, 1980

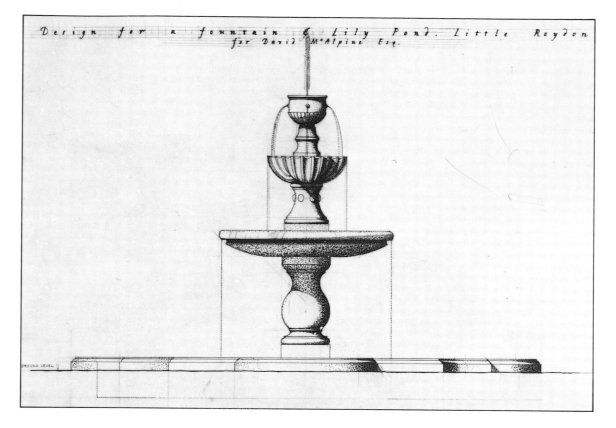

114. Little Roydon: fountain and lily pond, 1977

bers's Chinese temple which was standing derelict in a wood near Amesbury Abbey in Wiltshire – but unfortunately the condition of the building was too far gone for this to be practicable.

The idea of a birdcage based on the two-domed Salute in Venice was carried out (Figure 124), but the finished result was shipped to grace the McAlpine office in Perth, Australia. It stands ten feet high, the scale being governed by the standard brass Corinthian capitals which were bought from a manufacturer's catalogue. The mouldings, balustrades, column shafts, pinnacles and pediments are limewood; also the base and steps. The cherubs, like the capitals, are of brass, the base of mahogany, and the 'walls' of stainless steel mesh. It is not, Terry explains, a simple model, because in reducing the scale the mouldings had to be simplified and redesigned. Twenty-four full-sized drawings had to be made. 'This was necessary,' as Terry explains, 'because there are two types of portico, two large domes, three types of lanterns, campaniles as well as balustrades at several levels complete with finials, scrolled buttresses and other ornaments.'

126

115. Little Roydon: Temple of Echo

Terry has also worked for Lord McAlpine's brother, the Hon. David McAlpine, altering his house at Little Roydon in Kent in 1978. He felt that the house was unquestionably Doric in character, but he gave it a Corinthian doorcase because he sensed Mr McAlpine to be a strongly Corinthian person.

At Little Roydon he also built a fountain of Portland stone – water flows out of a goblet through four channels into a shell, overflows that into a basin, then drops into the lily pond in which the fountain stands – and a Portland stone seat with pediment and niches, based on William Kent's Pope's Seat in Cirencester Park. It has a Doric order with Baroque rusticated blocks.

More recently at Fawley House, Hampshire, Terry has for the same client created a rich architectural space out of what has been a long and gloomy corridor, only six feet wide, which faced you as you went through the front door. He did so by introducing a full-height Corinthian order, arches, and a minor Doric order flanking the doors (Figure 118). With a little false perspective as well, the effect is intended to recall Palladio's Teatro Olimpico in Vicenza.

127

118. Fawley House: hallway

FACING: *116. Higham: library with* trompe-l'œil *decoration (top)*
117. Thenford: interior of the summerhouse (bottom)

119. West Green: bridge and aviary

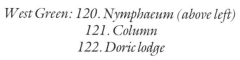

West Green: 120. Nymphaeum (above left)
121. Column
122. Doric lodge

123. Nymphaeum through Moon Gate

124. Salute birdcage

129. Thenford: summerhouse, side niche

130. Thenford: summerhouse

131. Thenford: bridge, 1980

132. West Wycombe: Temple of Venus, detail of order

133. West Wycombe: grotto below Temple of Venus

134. West Wycombe: Temple of Venus (facing)

135. Thenford: summerhouse, elevation and plan, 1982

THE THENFORD SUMMERHOUSE

Another client whose personality seemed without question to demand the Corinthian order was Michael Heseltine, the former Defence Secretary, who commissioned a summerhouse overlooking the swimming pool at his house Thenford House, near Banbury, in 1979. Mr Heseltine's wife, Anne, was already devoted to the Veneto and wanted a building that would recall the architecture there. Also the Heseltines had, before coming to Thenford, considered rescuing Heveningham Hall in Suffolk – the house by Taylor and Wyatt that had at that stage just passed to a reluctant Department of the Environment. Having fallen in love with the Heveningham orangery, they hoped that something of this would go into their summerhouse. Then when Terry visited Thenford, he was struck by the use of two different types of stone in the building – a hard grey stone like Portland (but in fact from North Oxfordshire) for the Doric doorcase and dressings, tawny Hornton stone for the walls.[2] These, then, were the starting points for the design. Despite the precedents, however, the summerhouse as it turned out is quite

2. Terry was interviewed about the Thenford summerhouse by Dan Cruickshank in the *Architects' Journal*, 14 December 1983.

138

different from anything that would have been done in the eighteenth century: it is a piece of late-twentieth-century Classicism – full of eclectic learning and carried off with enormous panache. When you see it, it appears – like Lutyens's buildings – smaller than you would expect from the photographs, for the columns are only ten foot six high. That it has the sense of scale and proportion of a large building is a tribute to its design.

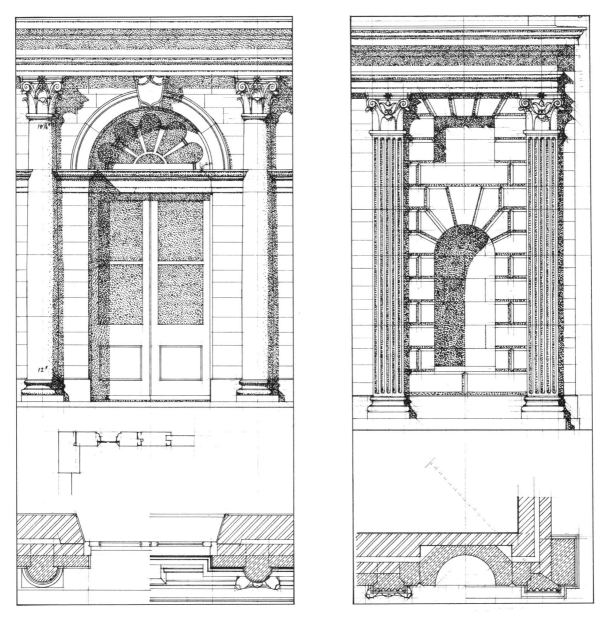

Thenford summerhouse: 136. Central door; 137. Side niche

It consists of one large room – forty feet by fifteen (the proportions eight to three) – with male and female changing cubicles and a kitchen behind. The architecture is therefore principally one façade. It faces south onto the grass terrace at the end of the pool, with a view of rolling fields beyond the hedge that keeps out the cows. This façade is full of complexities. The order, which has more a lily leaf than an acanthus, is reminiscent of Sanmicheli, and in its flatness may look debased to English eyes. Both smooth half-engaged columns and fluted pilasters are used, making virtually two orders. The half-engaged columns stand beneath the pediment, the pilasters flank the single bays at either end; and the spacing of the columns and pilasters reduces towards the ends – the central columns are six feet apart, the side ones five feet, the pilasters four feet. Moreover, in the five central bays are tall sash-windows that go down to the ground, to let in plenty of sunshine and fresh air in the summer. But to either end, in a sudden jump of scale, is a niche set amid rustication. As a precedent for the contrast in texture and scale at the end of the façade, Terry cites Palladio's Palazzo Valmarana in Vicenza.

The arches to the windows have three degrees of decoration – plain keystones at the ends, keystones with scrolls next to them, a keystone with the Heseltine shield in the centre – and the archivolts and imposts similarly progress from plain to moulded. And there is further richness in the shape of the urns on the skyline: those on the corners are square in section, rather than round, because they relate to the rectilinear pilasters below. The effect of the whole is either Mannerist or Baroque, according to your definition: perhaps on balance Mannerist because the façade which is charged with so much detail and movement remains essentially flat. Another ingredient of the façade is the use of five flutes to the pilasters. Seven would have been more usual, but five is common in Florence and any more would have looked too fussy on a building as small as the summerhouse.

So there is a lot to think about, if you feel so inclined, as you dry off on the terrace after your swim. But for those who do not choose to analyse the architecture in detail there is another, more sensuous element to which the intellectual games are subordinate: this is colour. At the moment, while it is new, we are lucky in being able to enjoy the Hornton stone in its primordial hues of green blotched with khaki: rather sadly, it will in time turn the reticent browny tweed colour of the house. (How amazing to think that all the eighteenth-century buildings in the region were once equally festive!) The Hornton stone contrasts with the pale, oat-coloured Clipsham, which is used for the architectural elements – columns, pilasters, dressings and urns. This has a slightly fluffy texture which

140

gives to the carving of the capitals a soft edge. One further point before going inside: the lantern over the door was provided in case there should be parties at night but the owners say that they have always felt that it obstructs the architecture, even if it does have a precedent above countless Mayfair front doors.

Inside, the geometrical, slate and Portland stone floor is derived from the Chiesa dei Gesuati in Venice and the fireplace with volutes from Ristorante Pozzo (a restaurant the Terrys happened to frequent) in Vicenza. Beams cross the ceiling, and beneath them are Ionic pilasters in *trompe-l'œil*. These were set out by Terry but painted by Marcus May, a former Guards officer, who also painted the trophies, medallions and landscapes round the walls. Perhaps the trophies are the most successful: they are on gardening and riding themes, and were inspired by the trophies of gardening implements, sprayed white, at the entrance of the Victoria and Albert Museum's 1979 'The Garden' exhibition. (Lord McAlpine has similar gardening trophies, but in three dimensions, in the conservatory at West Green.) The landscapes showing the estate, which are if anything too convincing, are seen as though through an arch: on one balustrade are the late Lanning Roper's notes for the gardener, on the other a squirrel eating the Erith and Terry bill.

Before leaving we must go outside again to look at the building's sides and back, which are plain and of pale pink and blue bricks. These are not show façades: by contrast to the sumptuousness of the main front, the model here seems to have been Paddington Green Church Hall.

CRICKET PAVILION, TEMPLE OF VENUS AND BRIDGE AT WEST WYCOMBE

Fancy does not always come dear. The first job that arrived in the office after Erith died was a cricket pavilion at West Wycombe, the superb eighteenth-century house in Buckinghamshire, owned by the National Trust and lived in by Sir Francis Dashwood. The cricket club had proposed buying a portable Scandinavian pavilion, but Sir Francis felt that they might do better than that, and the National Trust, whose historic buildings panel would have to pass the design, suggested Terry. As some timber could be had from the estate he explored the theme of the primitive hut, specifying columns made of rough-hewn tree-trunks with the bark still on them. Second-hand pantiles were used to cover a larchpole roof. There are Gothick windows at the sides, and the entrance from the veranda to the home

141

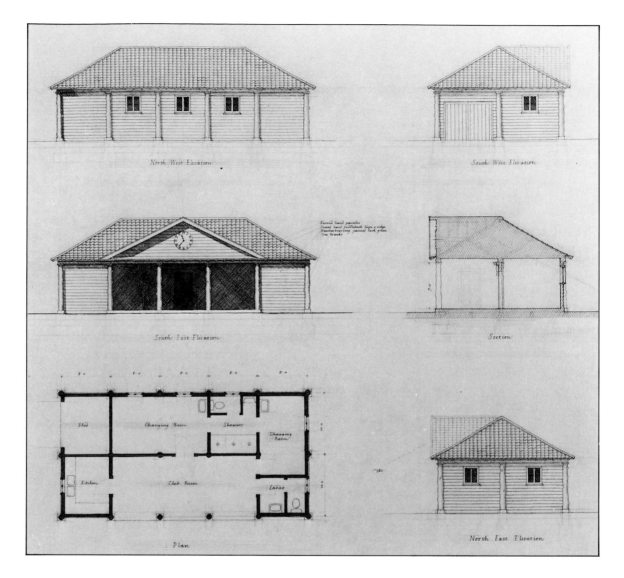

138. West Wycombe: cricket pavilion

team's changing room has an Egyptian temple front doorcase, with consoles bearing half-engaged cricket balls either side. Three solid wooden panels were made to fit between the columns of the veranda to close the building against vandals when not in use; unfortunately these are so heavy that there is a temptation only to take down the centre panel except for the most important matches. Sir Francis is contemplating replacing the panels with up-and-over garage-type doors.

Terry's next undertaking at West Wycombe, the Temple of Venus, has been very different in character. Many paintings in the house show the landscape park as it was in the day of Sir Francis's namesake, the second baronet, Baron le Despencer, who was not only a prime mover of the Society of Dilettanti but the founder of the notorious Hell Fire Club. It was well stocked with garden buildings, one of which was a temple on a mound to the west of the lake. Dedicated to Venus, the temple was the culminating point of an elaborate topography based on the female body, and both within and without were statues of similar erotic meaning. The present Sir Francis has set about re-creating the Temple of Venus and some of the other follies, although Terry's temple, as may be imagined, is a chaster affair than the original. It is a sparkling ornament, white as ivory when seen from a distance, in a glade of mature trees.

Sir Francis and Lady Dashwood themselves dug out the chalk block foundations of the original temple, which was found to have been oval. Beneath they also uncovered the oval cave, reached by an oval opening. In addition a drawing thought to be by Servandoni exists of Venus's Parlour, the area in front of the temple. The temple probably had twelve columns, and this was the number chosen by Terry. Following the old foundations Terry's design is elliptical, dimensioned according to the Pythagorean ellipse (see page 75). If the peristyle was a tease to detail, the result is also something of a tease

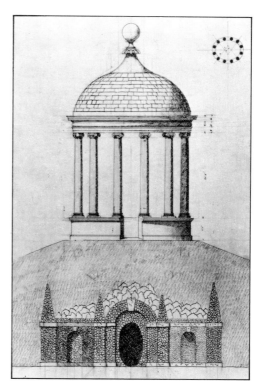

to the spectator, who is unlikely to realize at first sight that the shape is not circular. Only when you walk towards the temple at an angle, when the perspective makes the pan-tiled roof look as though it has been made out of rubber and pulled sideways, do you begin to appreciate the form. For the order, Terry used a simplified Ionic which has the abacus flush with the echinus, so it could almost be Doric if you imagined away the volutes. Both shafts and capitals are made of reconstituted stone, as is appropriate in a garden building; and the ball on top was constructed of fibre-glass by Jackson's. The remains of the old grotto were incorporated into a new design, with sweeping sides of flintwork and four obelisks.

Work at West Wycombe continues. The latest project was to reconstruct the Walton

139. West Wycombe: Temple of Venus

Bridge, shown in a painting by William Hannan of 1748. It was named after one built by the master carpenter and bridge specialist William Etheridge at Walton-on-Thames, which was then thought to have been the longest span bridge of wood in Europe. Although there were three arches in the centre the design employed only straight pieces of timber, which were set at tangents to the heads of the arches; this meant that any one member could be replaced without disrupting the whole. The bridge at Walton was demolished in 1780, so in pursuit of a crib Terry measured Etheridge's surviving mathematical bridge at Queens' College, Cambridge. He also saw a bridge that suited the site rather better at Iffley Lock and measured that too. Terry does not believe in starting from scratch when he can take a lesson from someone else's efforts at doing the same thing. 'I would not take all the credit for it,' Terry says of the West Wycombe bridge, 'but I still think it looks very good.' Since the original Walton Bridge was replaced by a solid structure, a new site for Terry's version had to be found. It was chosen by Sir Francis's son Edward and the new structure will be named the Edward Bridge, having been opened on his twenty-first birthday.

Sir Francis intends his next project to be the rebuilding of the brick and flint façade to the boathouse, which is seen in a painting of 1781.

STABLES AT EYDON HALL

Terry's work at the stables of Eydon Hall in Northamptonshire for Mr Gerald Leigh is satisfying because of the simple and elegant solution of a practical problem. The turn-of-the-century owners of the hall had been friends of Sir Herbert Baker, who had built a handsome stable range entered by a triumphal arch, housing tack room and loft, with the loose boxes in two quadrant wings. The wings were of wood and, charmingly, had Tuscan columns painted on; but they also had a flat roof, which was leaking, and the ventilation was poor. There was also no covered area for grooming, rubbing down, harnessing and so on. Terry's proposal was to put on a pitched roof and bring it forward onto columns. This provided a secure roof, gave the horses more air, gave an overhang beneath which work could be done in wet weather – and introduced a proper three-dimensional Tuscan order. It also had the benefit, for what it is worth, of preserving Sir Herbert's work, and therefore saved money on what a complete rebuilding might have cost.

140 and 141. Stables at Eydon Hall

142. Dufours Place, 1983 (linocut)

CHAPTER NINE

OFFICES AND GENTLEMEN

It is to some extent Terry's bugbear that he has become well known as an architect of country houses and allied buildings. Not that he does not enjoy the country-house work – he does, enormously. When you work for a rich private client price is not necessarily the first consideration, so there are more possibilities for pure architecture: for columns, pediments, archivolts, imposts and brackets. But his good fortune in this respect has led some critics to accuse him of dilettantism. They say that Classicism would get a bad mauling if it tried to compete in the market place. They repeat the misconceptions cited at the beginning of Chapter 4. Therefore the commission to build a speculative office block for Haslemere Estates plc in the centre of London – off Broadwick Street, Soho – was seized by Terry as a particularly welcome opportunity to show how Classicism and traditional building methods are not played out; that they can offer very significant benefits to the developer, as well as to the ultimate users of the offices. Office development is, architecturally, about the toughest market place there is.

Terry's office block, Dufours Place, has been a success. When it was begun in the spring of 1982 there were already several signboards up in Broadwick Street advertising offices to let. When it was completed eighteen months later, many of those same signboards were still there. But Dufours Place was let before it was even finished. Not all the accommodation was in fact office space: as with most developments, the planners had insisted on a mix of uses which included a car park, a light industrial area, a doctor's surgery and twenty-five flats (which again sold before work had finished). With its traditional brick walls and sash-windows, Dufours evidently had the right image for the directors of the companies which have gone there. It also immediately gave the impression of being a sympathetic place in which to live and work. Not having to wait for the block to let was of considerable benefit to the developers. A delay in letting can involve a developer in a double burden, as he both loses potential rents and has to continue to pay interest on capital.

Those who argue that Terry's Classicism is uneconomic forget that there are many different elements that go to make up a building's cost. One of them that is crucial to office development, for instance, is the time spent waiting to receive planning consent. In the last five years the planning controls affecting historic buildings and conservation areas have been markedly tightened up. While this may not at first sight appear to affect new buildings, in fact it does, very considerably. For virtually all sites in the centres of busy cities have historic buildings implications. It is highly probable that the new building will be in a conservation area, or next to a listed building, or in a street regarded as of special group value – even if the demolition of protected fabric is not proposed. The old Modernist argument that the texture of an historic urban area is the result of many different generations each having built in 'the style of the age', regardless of the one before, and that therefore an out-of-scale block in modern materials would mix-and-

143. Dufours Place: frontispiece

match perfectly well in a street of old houses, has largely gone out of fashion. Planners have become much more likely to insist that the new work should be in keeping with the old. This has not always been to the good of architecture. Too often it has led to a watering-down of a design which can be worse – through total blandness – than the over-aggressive first proposal. But it has had a very positive effect on the encouragement of Classical architecture. The roles have been reversed. Developers now increasingly find that a proposal in traditional materials, with broken surfaces giving a human sense of scale, will jump planning hurdles more quickly than a lumbering monolith handicapped by a dead weight of concrete and glass. Classicism is only one among a number of traditional, or pseudo-traditional, styles to have benefited from the change: another is neo-Vernacular. But the effect on Classicism has been the more dramatic because chances have appeared where they seemed never to have existed before.

It was through conservation that Terry was introduced to office work. The site for Dufours Place lay behind a row of derelict Georgian buildings. They were not so different – except for their condition – from Downing Street, and Terry was called upon to advise on the details of their restoration and conversion to offices. It was felt that it would be more attractive to have the residential accommodation in the more secluded back area of the development, Dufours Place, rather than on a noisy Soho street. From the repair and conversion of the houses, Terry

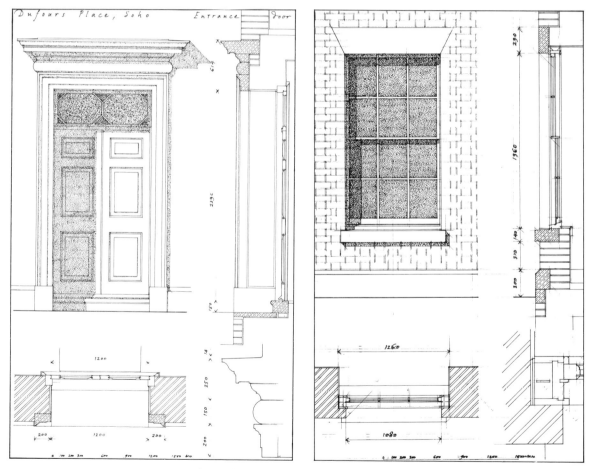

Dufours Place: 144. Doorcase; 145. Window

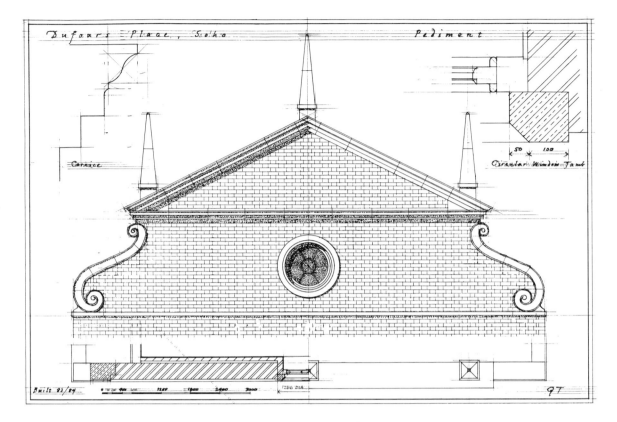

146. Dufours Place: pediment

progressed to the design of the new building for offices and flats. Haslemere asked Terry to build high. They had purchased the site with an existing consent for offices of the floor area ultimately provided; but the consent was based on a scheme which envisaged an eight-storey glass and concrete block. Terry stuck to eight storeys (including basement). But by contrast his office block is of the traditional London building material: load-bearing brick. Of course, this had been, of necessity, used everywhere in the eighteenth century, when the only alternative was building with wood. But so thoroughly was load-bearing brick replaced in the nineteenth and twentieth centuries by steel and, later, reinforced concrete that the quantity surveyor for the job regarded it as revolutionary. Far safer, he said, to use a tried and tested material like reinforced concrete. As it happened, the tenders for the job came in well under estimate.

The use of load-bearing brick in a modern office block is what makes Dufours Place special. As a number of architects have been finding since the 1960s, there are strong arguments in favour of the material. Since it has been around for

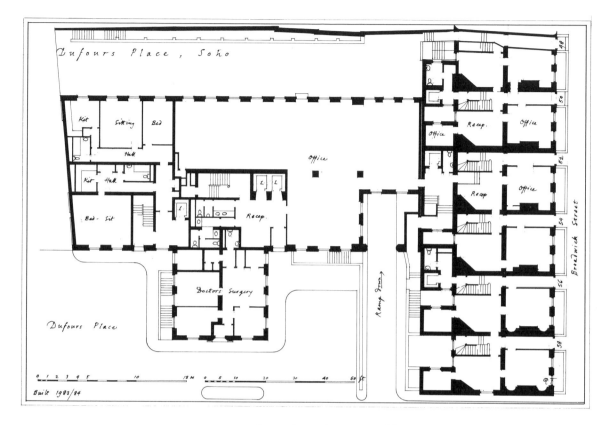

147. Dufours Place: plan, ground floor

literally thousands of years, far more is known about it than about new materials and modern technology (see Chapter 11). This has a practical import for the architect as well as the client, given the enormous damages an architect is liable to in cases of building failure – or even the exorbitant costs of liability insurance for architects regarded as bad risks. Brick can even work out as a cheaper form of construction than reinforced concrete: only one trade – that of the bricklayer – is involved and so continuity of work (in case of strikes, late delivery and so on) is more easily achieved. But load-bearing brick construction is slower and the thick walls – massively thick on the ground floor – cut down on the vital gross to net floor ratios. Gross is the figure on which planning consent is given, and is measured from the outside of the building; net represents everything that is left over within the walls after staircases and services have been allowed for. It is the net area on which the developer makes his profit, and to lose part of it in wall thicknesses is a serious matter. Here Terry's year in the C. H. Elsom office stood him in good stead by enabling him to contrive a highly efficient internal plan to compensate; and happily Haslemere, a well-established company with a reputation at the higher end of the market, do not see the maximization of profits as incompatible with achieving a high standard of architecture.

Dufours Place was not quite Terry's first experience of office building, since he had worked with Erith on 10 South Square in Gray's Inn, built in 1971–2 shortly before Erith's death. This provided principally a common room, but also robing rooms, students' rooms, flats and offices – accommodation not very different in its requirements from that of an office block. 10 South Square had, similarly, been built of load-bearing brick, although, at five storeys (including basement), it was three storeys shorter than Dufours Place. Also, because 10 South Square had been built with a knowledge of how it would eventually be used, it was divided into rooms: Dufours Place had to be open-plan – although the occupiers have in many cases subdivided the space into rooms. Both 10 South Square and Dufours Place have concrete floors. Concrete has positive advantages for floors in buildings used by many people, since it cuts down noise and is also impenetrable to water (in the case of bath overflows and so on). The eight storeys of Dufours Place are 'about as high as you can go without losing the commonsense values of Classicism,' Terry believes. 'You can just manage if the lifts pack up.' [1] It is a height that can be seen throughout Amsterdam, for example, or in Georgian warehouses in London, Liverpool and Bristol. Build any higher in load-bearing brick and the thickness of the ground-floor walls – already two foot seven and a half inches at Dufours Place – becomes impracticably great.

Whereas 10 South Square, replacing an Edwardian building, had had a clear, unimpeded site, which allowed a broad front with a pediment (as well as some 'instant history' in the glazing bars and the Gothick buttery adjoining the genuinely Gothic chapel), the site of Dufours Place is a cramped back area in Soho. There was no room for expansiveness. It is not possible to step back and take the building in as a whole, from the centre of the façade. It can only be seen as a piece from a sharp angle. Hence the cruciform plan – which works both visually and as a means of getting as much light as possible into the rooms. In office building there is little spare money for architecture, beyond, in Terry's case, load-bearing brick walls, sash-windows, stone quoins and a slate roof. So Dufours Place is largely utilitarian. The Georgian building type that most approximates to an office block is a warehouse, and that is essentially what Dufours Place is. To make it a little more than a warehouse, however, it has a Dutch gable, a cupola (concealing ventilation plant) and a Baroque doorcase with a dash of false

1. Quoted from *The Times*, ibid.

152

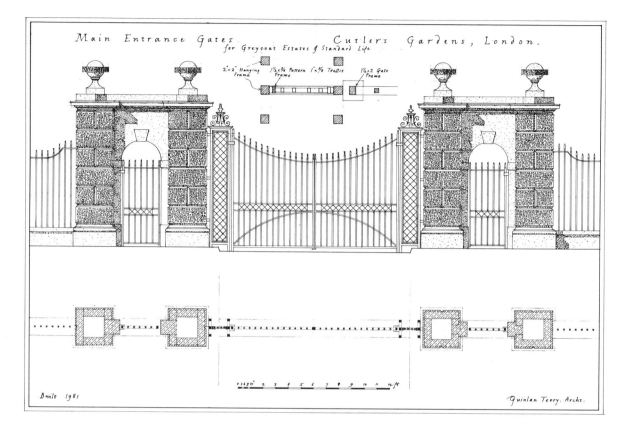

148. Cutlers Gardens: main entrance gates

perspective, in stone, in three receding arches above. The front door to the building deserved the prominence awarded it by the doorcase, and false perspective is a remarkably low-cost means of giving glamour.

Given that Dufours Place is virtually a warehouse, it is not surprising that a genuine Georgian warehouse can be made successfully into an office block. In 1982 Greycoat Estates working with Standard Life Assurance approached Terry to convert the two remaining warehouses in the Cutlers Gardens complex near Liverpool Street Station. In 1978 the future Cutlers Gardens – then known as the Cutler Street warehouses – became a conservationists' *cause célèbre*. Behind gaunt, impenetrable façades lay four and a half acres of bonded warehouses built, from 1769 onwards, by England's most famous commercial venture, the East India Company. Their historical importance was great, and so was their architectural value. The first blocks were built by the East India Company's surveyor Richard Jupp, one of an architectural dynasty who worked mostly in the city. But in 1799 Jupp was succeeded by no less an architect than Henry Holland. It is thought that

153

he designed the tremendous zigzag façade to Middlesex Street, which conservationists saw as the crux of the entire site. Greycoat Estates and Standard Life had employed R. Seifert and Partners to design a 'conversion' scheme, which involved demolishing all the great Middlesex Street elevation and stripping the interiors of such blocks as had been retained. Listed building consent and planning permission had already been obtained by another company for another scheme.[2] Greycoat Estates and Standard Life declined to modify the Seifert proposals, despite an appeal made by Mark Girouard and other architectural historians who flew to Edinburgh, where Standard Life have their headquarters, in an aeroplane specially chartered for the purpose. However the attitude towards conservation in the City Planning Office had hardened in the six years since 1978, and the developers themselves, who had always in theory promoted the idea of a conservationist scheme, felt able to preserve more of the two small warehouses which survived. Terry came on the scene when he was asked to design the new gates.

He was then given the job of converting Bengal House (or 20 New Street), parallel to New Street, and 9A Devonshire Square, which is at right angles. They were built about 1790. In the buildings converted by Seifert, only the brick outer walls and the window openings were retained. But the fact is that Bengal House and 9A Devonshire Square, which have been standing for almost two hundred years, were so massively built that they have at least another two hundred years left in them. Therefore Terry, unlike Seifert, has kept the thick timber floors, which offer more than adequate loadings for office use, and the cast-iron doors, columns and window openings.

The character of the buildings is brute strength, and Terry has played on it. Going into Bengal House is a little like experiencing one of Piranesi's *Carceri*. The spaces are huge and the textures rough, as they have always been. The walls have been left exposed brick. Vast timber beams are also exposed: it is perfectly acceptable to keep them from a fire regulations point of view because, being so thick, they burn through slowly. Where new elements of architecture have been introduced, as in the great Bramante-esque arch of the entrance hall and the

2. *Un peu d'histoire.* When the Cutler Street site had been sold by the Port of London Authority in 1976, it was bought by the property developers English Continental. Listed building consent was given for a new hall and offices for the Baltic Exchange, which had threatened to leave London for Hamburg – taking with them over £100 million of invisible earnings – if new premises were not found quickly. A clause was included in the consent that the new development should be used for not less than five years only by the Baltic Exchange and its member companies. But partly because its present building in St Mary Axe was listed, which reduced its potential value, the Baltic never moved. Nevertheless, Greycoat/ Standard Life were permitted to make full use of the consent.

large-scale stone staircase with its splendid Renaissance balusters (derived from the Basilica at Vicenza) to the first flight, they are appropriately massive in feeling. Also, intriguingly, the Doric order found in some of the columns has been continued in the ground-floor rooms. An advantage of using an order is that pipes and cables can be hidden in the beams (in fact hollow) that they appear to support. As the staircase winds its way up through six floors, the balustrade becomes iron and to a Chinese Chippendale design: a handsome answer to the regulation that no sphere four inches across (big enough for a child's head) can be allowed to penetrate the gaps. This metal balustrade serves a double function, because it also acts as a truss to strengthen the cantilevered stone steps which had grown unacceptably weak. Electric wires are concealed in the handrail to light the elegant swan-necked lanterns. Terry has designed the entrance gates to the whole complex.

The tough attitude on conservation that led to Terry's involvement at Bengal House is itself evidence of the low ebb to which some Modernist doctrines had fallen. The token conservation of parts of old buildings is now no longer thought enough: old buildings must be preserved in as many of their parts as is possible. People have rebelled against the Modernist alternative. A building of 1790 – even a warehouse – is recognized as having an almost prelapsarian quality. It was built before architecture had lost its way. And Terry's work makes another point. There is no reason why conservation should, given the necessary talent, knowledge and respect on the part of the architect, be a cramp on creativity.

149. Dufours Place: entrance

150. Dufours Place (facing)

151. *Dufours Place: cupola*   152. *Dufours Place: detail of staircase*

153. Cutlers Gardens: main entrance gates   154. Cutlers Gardens: turntable gates

155. Bengal House: entrance hall

Bengal House

New Balustrade & Lanterns to Existing Stairs

0 1 2 3 4 5 6 7 8 9'   2 M

Built 1985   Quinlan Terry Archt

156. Bengal House: foyer and wall light (top left)
157. Bengal House: balustrade and lanterns (top right and below)

158. Bengal House: entrance gates

159. Bengal
House: yard

160. Bengal
House: steps

161. Bengal House: interior

FACING *162. Bengal House: plan*

163. Bengal House: screen and steps

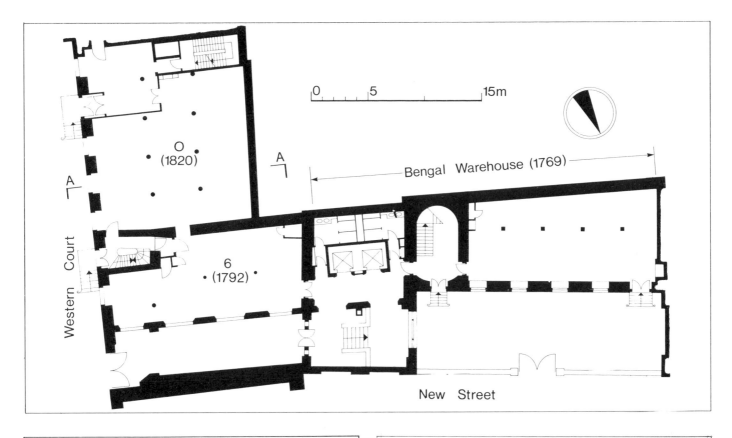

O
(1820)

A

Bengal Warehouse (1769)

Western Court

6
(1792)

0   5   15m

A

New Street

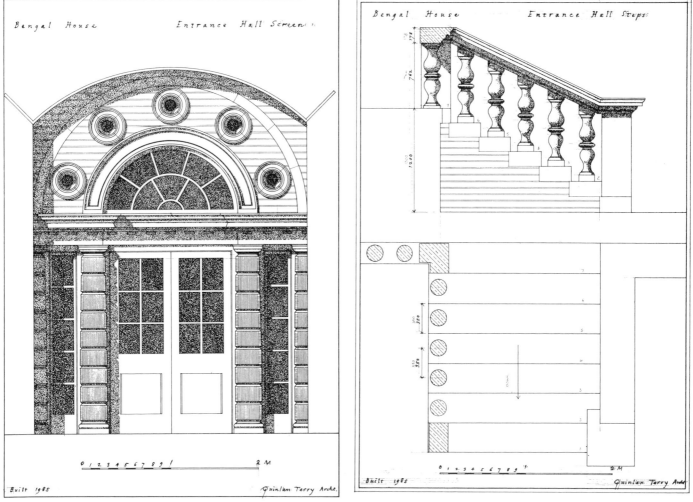

Bengal House   Entrance Hall Screen

Built 1985   Quinlan Terry Archt.

0 1 2 3 4 5 6 7 8 9 1   2 M

Bengal House   Entrance Hall Steps

Built 1985   Quinlan Terry Archt.

0 1 2 3 4 5 6 7 8 9 1   2 M

167. A Greek Doric capital for Richmond Riverside, seen at the Empire Stone works, Leicester, where it was made. Like those in the Turban Development at Woodbridge, it is composed of reconstituted stone. The casting process is highly skilled.

FACING: *164. Woodbridge: shopfront, Doric columns (top left)*

165. Gray's Inn: kiosk (top right)

166. Woodbridge: shopfront (bottom)

168. St Mary's Church, Paddington Green: organ case

CHAPTER TEN

THE OFFICE

Terry's own office in Dedham High Street is not on the Herculean scale of Bengal House. It exists in two timber-framed cottages – originally Elizabethan – with a honeycomb of rooms. In the eighteenth century the cottages were faced with ochre-washed stucco which is peeling off in places, and in the early twentieth century they were made into a little rural telephone exchange – hence the name, Old Exchange. The front door is low, beneath an overhang, and when Terry opens the door to you his tall, suited figure fills the frame. His own office is the one Erith had: the staff spontaneously moved his equipment in there when Erith died, in a gesture of *le roi se meurt, vive le roi*. The walls are papered with time-darkened pages of *The Times*. They are probably kept out of a feeling of piety, but it would be impossible to replace them, of course, now that the personal columns have disappeared from the front page. There is a good mahogany desk, a drawing table, an electric bar fire and a shelf of source-books and sketchbooks. With the increase of work since Richmond Riverside the office has expanded to fill every available space in the building: with its little doorways and crooked passages and precipitous staircases, its rooms in the attic and at the back, Old Exchange is a brilliant example of organic growth – or Dickensian jumble, if you prefer. Which only proves the rule that no architect inhabits the kind of building he gives his clients. The critic Martin Pawley found his visit 'an amazing experience'.[1]

Not only is the office physically unlike that of other firms but, since the practice requires different skills, it is organized somewhat differently, too. The key to the regime is suggested in a letter written by Erith to Terry about a rich client who was supposed to take up arms against a planning refusal. 'He has in fact done nothing – probably been skiing. (I have worker's contempt for the laziness of the pleasure loving rich, always skiing or in Scotland or Morocco or the Barbados or looking at Palladio's Villas or losing weight at Eaton Hall, never there.)' Terry,

---

1. He interviewed Terry in the *Guardian*, 1 May 1985.

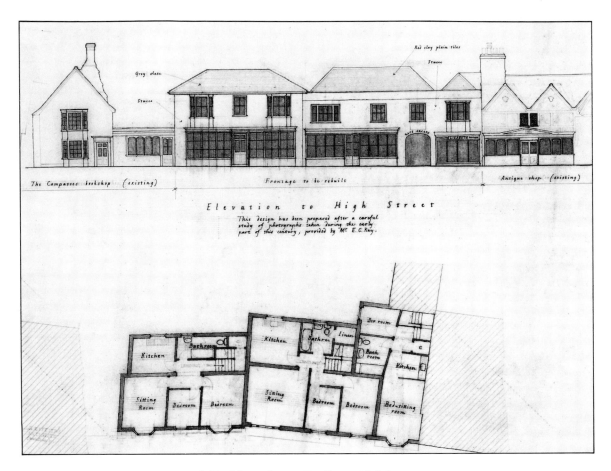

169. Alterations to Dedham High Street

like Erith, operates on the opposite principle to that of 'never there'. Although, recently, he has necessarily had to travel to meetings and site visits one or two days a week, he rarely stays away. Even more rarely does he go down to London for lectures, clubs or other professional get-togethers. He does not encourage visits to his office by those not directly concerned with his practice. He believes in the virtue of steady hard work. 'Designing anything is a lengthy business with us,' he wrote in the Kingswalden Notes. 'No genius stuff here of the Maestro rushing it off with breathtaking originality in the heat of the moment. It's always one long concentrated effort which one has to attend to without distraction & even then there is a good risk of it being a failure.'

Terry goes through the whole warren of rooms twice a day, making a tour of the drawing boards. There is also an out-station with four boards at his own house, Higham Hall. The first idea for a design tends to be worked out on foolscap sheets

170

in the evening when Terry is at home, by the fire. He likes to formulate the first idea fairly quickly and to pass on a sketch to the client. There is no point in doing more at this stage, he says, because his first thoughts may be quite different from what the client has in mind. If the design is taken further, however, it goes through an endless process of refinement with the assistants in the office. Terry described the working method when Erith was alive in the Kingswalden Notes:

We always talk – endlessly – & then draw out the conclusions. We are usually dissatisfied with the result so we go on talking around the problem, mainly about commonsense construction & historical precedent. At this point a good deal of book searching takes place including cribbing from sketch books & walks down the High St. to see how it should be done. Eventually by a combination of discussion and drawing a solution is arrived at.

That process has remained much the same, the discussion involving each assistant to a greater or lesser extent depending on their abilities. The sourcebooks have changed little (see Chapter 2) – Palladio, Sanmicheli, Longhena, Bramante, Letarouilly and Batty Langley. Once the basic shape of the design has been decided on, Terry will put the details through limitless revisions which only the junior staff have the patience to redraw so many times. Then the design will be passed over to the senior staff at tender stage to finalize the technical details and co-ordinate levels, structure, damp proof courses and services.

About twenty people work in the office. At the top of the hierarchy is the vitally important figure of Hugh Barrell, Terry's associate who has been with the firm for forty years. His family have lived in Dedham for generations, and he is the key man on site. His immense experience of choosing wood and stone, and of rejecting workmanship which is not up to standard, is an essential factor behind the unsurpassed finish of Terry's buildings, as it had been of Erith's. When talking to builders he is frequently heard to use old East Anglian sayings like 'two wrongs don't make a right' and 'if you think that, you could think anything'. With the firm's reputation for firm dealing, builders are less likely to try to palm Erith and Terry off with bad work. It is a rare and, as Terry explains, invaluable asset, which not only ensures a high standard of building but keeps the firm out of the liability courts. Now Hugh's son Roger is also at work in the firm.

Like Terry most of the staff live locally, and with only a five-minute drive to work, the long hours do not seem so onerous as they might do in London. The high standards of Erith's day are still expected, most noticeably in draughts-manship. Terry believes that this sense of quality explains the dedication and enthusiasm that motivate the office. There is only one man ultimately responsible for designing buildings, and that is Terry – as it had been Erith in Erith's day. The success of this system depends on choosing staff who do not feel frustrated that their involvement in the design is at the practical level. Their approach tends to be that of the craftsman, and often they are recruited from local builders and joiners. Terry would far rather have someone who is good with his hands than a man with a degree from architectural school.

It is often said that first-rate craftsmen no longer exist, but Terry finds that in most instances this is not true. They can be found – though you may have to pay for them. Over the years Erith and Terry have established a special relationship with a number of East Anglian firms, who offer both a better and a rather cheaper service than he could find in London. For stone they often use Collins and Curtis of Ipswich. The best builder for miles around used to be W.T. Wheeler of East Bergholt: they built Erith's Great House in Dedham in 1938, and Edward Dale, one of Erith and Terry's senior staff, began as an estimator with them. Alas, they had to close down owing to lack of good work in 1978. But many of their best men went to Taylor's of Bildeston and it has thus been possible for the connection with Erith and Terry to survive. The other builder in East Bergholt was William Aldous and Son. Peter Aldous carried on the family firm for twenty years and then, as building became more catalogue-bound, his original architectural training led him to close the firm and join Erith and Terry in 1967. A preferred joiner is Mabbits of Colchester. They were 'trained' by Stephen Dykes-Bower to do Gothic work, and of course their skills are equally adaptable to Classicism. But, if you are unused to this professionalism, it comes as a surprise to find a Gothic crocket next to a Corinthian capital when you visit their shop. For ironwork Terry likes to go to Jim Smith

169. St Mary's, Paddington Green: organ case 1976

in Ardleigh, the next village: it is satisfactory to have a blacksmith called Smith.

Despite the greater activity of recent years, the office has retained its versatile, country character; and the strongest impression to be taken away from an afternoon spent in the office looking at Erith and Terry drawings is the quantity of work that has been designed, if not in every case built. As one after another of the big sheets of tracing paper is rolled back, one sees cottages, swimming pool alterations, designs for offices, for golf clubs, for the racing world, numerous house alterations, new bookcases for a friend. Two types of work should be mentioned here because they will not be elsewhere: restoration and churches. Both are time-consuming and labour-intensive, and tend to be overlooked in accounts of Terry's work. Terry's biggest restoration project was Queen's College, Oxford, which was the subject of a controversy pursued in *Popular Archaeology*

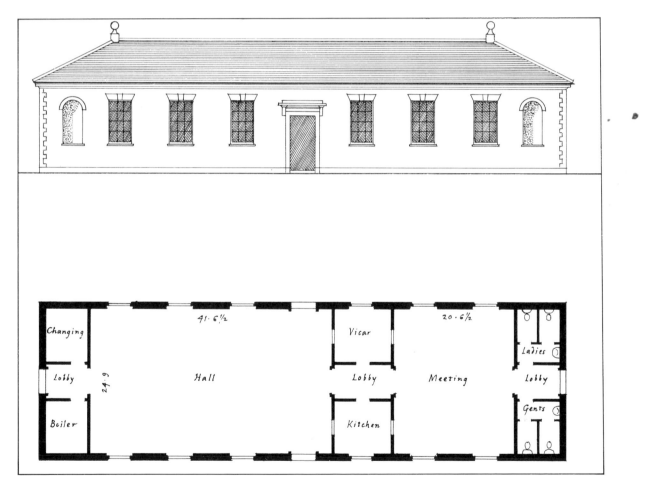

171. St Mary's Church, Paddington Green: hall

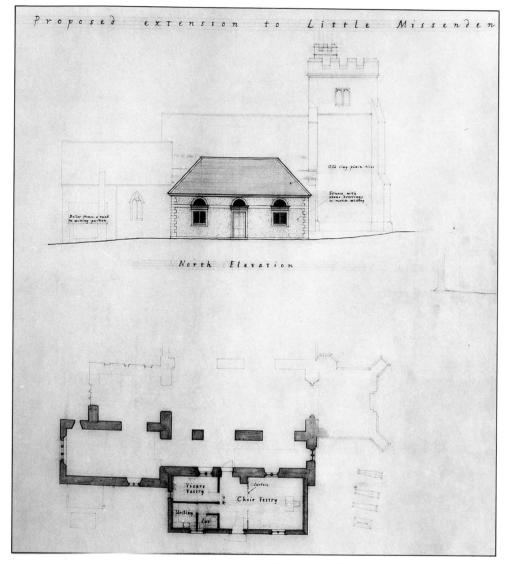

172. Little Missenden Church: additions

from March to August 1983.[2] This turned on an academic's assertion that column bases on the north façade of Front Quad were not Bath stone, used in a Victorian restoration, but one of the local stones used by the original Georgian architect.- Terry, having so often worked with Bath stone in the Bryanston sculptorium, knew perfectly well how to recognize it when he saw it; so did his masons, J. Joslin (Contractors) Ltd, who have worked with stonework in Oxford for several

2. See *Popular Archaeology*, March 1983, and correspondence in May and August 1983; also the *Guardian*, 15 February 1983.

generations. Analysis of petrographic sections by the Building Research Station proved that the stone did indeed come from the Bath area, as those with practical experience had been convinced all along. The work at Queen's also involved repairing and repainting the Georgian chapel, which Terry found a specially congenial part of the job.

As for the churches, the demand here has been to create rooms where After Service Fellowship can take place. At Little Missenden a modest brick box was added to the Gothic church. To Terry, this solution is doubly satisfying since it combines a sense of the House of Joy (see page 11) and a bit of instant history. A new church hall was built at St Mary's, Paddington Green, in 1976. Here, the church itself had already been restored in Erith's time with money gained in compensation for the enlargement of West Way. Then in 1978 a superb organ-case was erected to Terry's design and dedicated to the memory of Erith. With its central and flanking towers, its cornice, scrolls and gadrooned and flaming urns, this was inspired by the organs in the churches at Wareham and Blandford in Dorset, which Terry knew from his Bryanston days. They were by the late-Georgian organ builder G. P. England, who was an exact contemporary of John Plaw who designed St Mary's in 1791. But the flaming urns and some of the other details were derived from a source closer to Terry's home: the Burkitt memorial in Dedham church, which Terry will say is 'as good as anything in Italy'.

173. Corinthian capital

CHAPTER ELEVEN

THE ORDERS AND
GENUINE CLASSICISM

When you meet Quinlan Terry his style seems the precise equivalent of his architecture. He dresses in understated, conservative, well-made English clothes. He lives in a solid, four-square, handsome Georgian house. When he speaks it is difficult not to be impressed by his clarity and reasonableness, which somewhat belie the epithet of 'God's architect' recently given in a newspaper article. For there is no Messianic gleam in the eye, no Bible-thumping, no attempt to convert the unconverted (except possibly to Classical architecture, and only then if you have already shown a marked predisposition to waver from alternative persuasions). Terry is too much in love with the practical business of architecture to be a crusader, at least in the office. But equally, the consonance between the different facets of his life and his architecture is not coincidental. It reflects a singularly complete and fully formed view of life, work, the world and God, in which there are no loose ends and few if any doubts. A central prop of this philosophy is that Classical architecture is 'good'. It makes you feel good; it is good of itself; it is good because, according to Terry, it is divinely inspired.

Wisely perhaps, Terry does not expect everyone to agree with his belief that the orders derive from instructions about building the Tabernacle that God gave to Moses when He revealed the Ten Commandments. But to the unconvinced he still offers his account as a parable of the spiritual content of Classical architecture, which *does something* to people'. Other fables about the origin of the orders are little more plausible: for instance Vitruvius's charming story of the Corinthian maid (who left a basket on top of a young acanthus plant, which was later observed to have grown up and entwined itself round it) or the Abbé Laugier's rustic hut (see page 123). And oddly – and Terry emphasizes, quite coincidentally – a similar idea can be found in the legends of Freemasonry. According to the lore

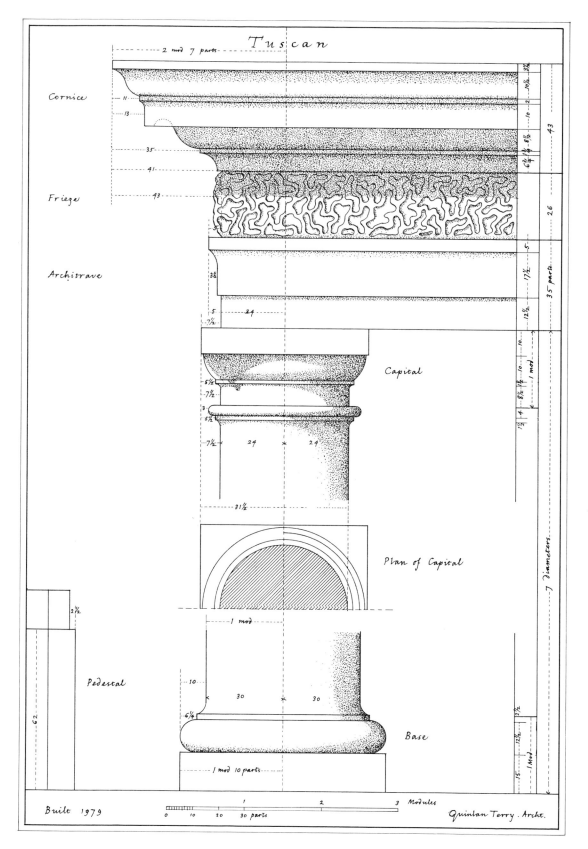

Tuscan

Cornice

Frieze

Architrave

Capital

Plan of Capital

Pedestal

Base

Built 1979

Quinlan Terry. Archt.

0 10 20 30 parts   1   2   3 Modules

174. Tuscan order

of the craft all geometry, and therefore the science of building, can be traced back to the teachings of Abraham, and it is from the secrets brought to Europe by men who had worked on the Temple that Classical architecture derives. Terry's theory was elaborated in the essay which won Terry the 1982 European Award for the Reconstruction of the City from the Philippe Rotthier Foundation in Paris (published in the *Architectural Review*, February 1983). But here I will quote from the more condensed version contained in 'Genuine Classicism', a lecture given at the Royal Institute of British Architects in November 1983 and published in the RIBA's *Transactions*.

When we were all at architectural schools we were taught that the Doric, Ionic and Corinthian orders originated in the Greek regions of Doria, Ionia and Corinth ... But in looking deeply into this subject we find that each nation has in fact copied the architectural details of the one it conquered, and as you know Alexander conquered the Persians in 332 BC. You can see at Persepolis to this day, large fluted columns with entasis, intricately carved bases with leaf and tongue and bead and reel enrichment, not to mention capitals of animals' heads with horns. At this time (before Alexander's conquest), the Greeks were putting up a very simple form of the Doric order as can be seen at the sixth century BC temple at Paestum.

And if we go further back we find that the Persians got their ideas from the Babylonians and the Egyptians. Now the Egyptians in their earlier dynasties, were only constructing simple geometrical forms like the pyramid and obelisk. It was not until Shishak that the more intricate

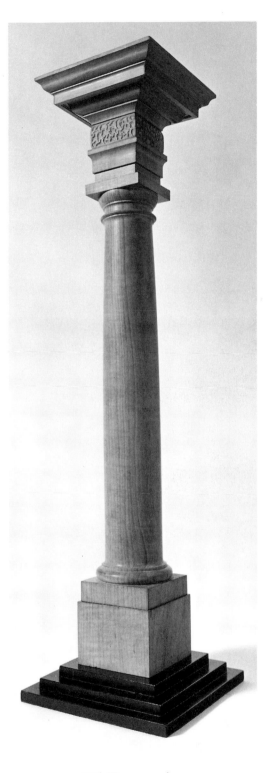

175. Tuscan order

179

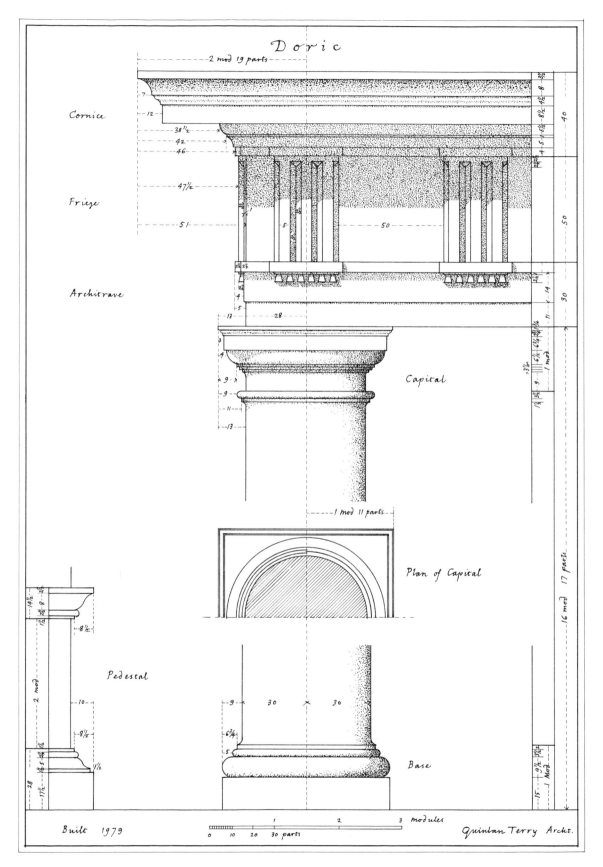

Doric

Cornice

Frieze

Architrave

Capital

Plan of Capital

Pedestal

Base

2 mod 19 parts

1 mod 11 parts

Built 1979

Quinlan Terry Archt.

1　　2　　3 modules

0　10　20　30 parts

176. Doric order

architectural details and ornaments were used. The importance of Shishak is very great because he was the king who attacked Jerusalem after King Solomon's death in about 950, and it is recorded in Holy Writ that he took away the ornaments of the temple. So this brings us back to the Temple of Solomon. Not only was this temple described in glowing terms by the Queen of Sheba, but it was also the talk of the ancient world. It was built to a strict classical plan, with its capitals made up of 'nets of checkerwork ... pomegranates ... ram's horns and ... lilywork' (1 Kings 7:16–22).

Theologians of every persuasion agree that this Temple building was derived directly from an earlier prototype, the Tabernacle in the Wilderness as described by Moses in the Book of Exodus 3,500 years ago – which makes it by far the earliest written specification of a building known to man. There is an outer court with pillars supporting the hangings. Inside there is a small, symmetrical, wooden building overlaid with gold with columns at the entrance and inside to divide the Holy place from the Holy of Holies.

It is not difficult to make a careful reconstruction of this description and compare it with the more elaborate and permanent construction of the Temple of Solomon. Thus one can draw up a version of the birth of these three orders of architecture.

The Doric order began as a post driven into the ground to support a primitive enclosure and held upright by guy ropes. It is then formalized by the inspired artist in the Court of the Tabernacle. The hangings are supported from hooks on rails from silver capitals with hooks and fillets on columns of acacia wood set in brass bases. This is later developed into the stone colonnade around the Temple Court, supporting cedarwood architrave under the beams, bracing principal rafters, plates, com-

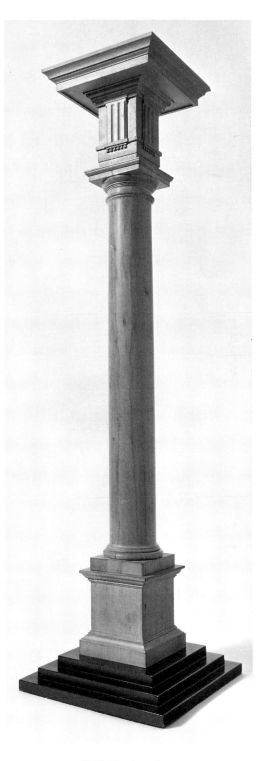

177. Doric order

181

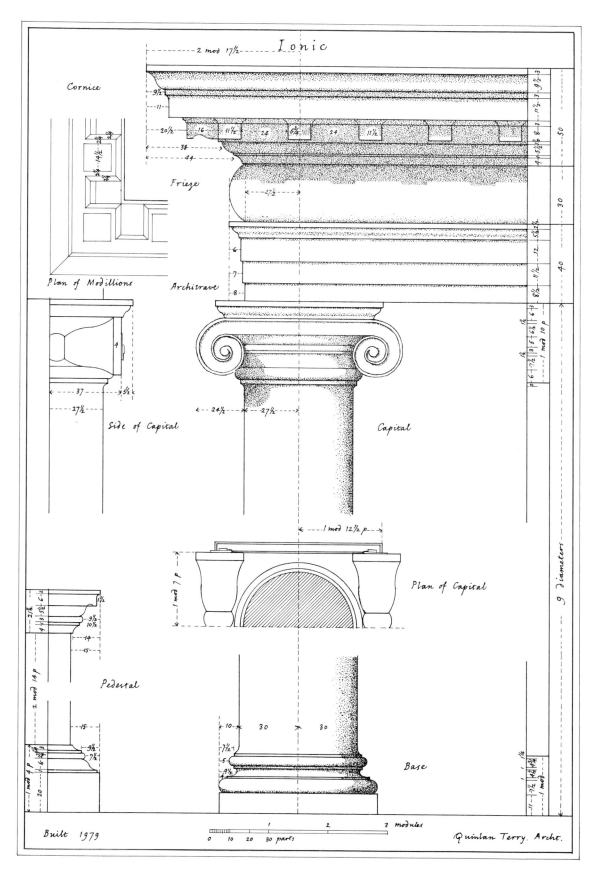

Ionic

Cornice

Plan of Modillions

Side of Capital

Frieze

Architrave

Capital

Plan of Capital

Pedestal

Base

9 Diameters

Built 1979

1   2   3 modules
0   10   20   30 parts

Quinlan Terry. Archt.

178. Ionic order

mon rafters and tilting fillets supporting a tile roof.

If you drive a green branch into the ground, it will sprout leaves. This happens easily with ash and willow in this country and the same happens to the palm tree in the Middle East. Thus the Ionic order combines this natural tendency with the imagery of the sacrificial ram's horns. Such capitals were placed upon columns at the door of the Tabernacle.

If a rope is tied below a sprouting palm branch, another layer of leaves will develop and curl under the square top, as in the Corinthian order at the entrance to the Holy of Holies. Solomon enriched it further with 'baskets of chequerwork' and festoons hanging from the rosettes in the abacus. [1]

The point is not so much whether Terry's theory is true – archaeologists might pepper it with holes – but that he believes it. Those who suspect that he is only doing it to tease are wrong. The significance of the theory to Terry is obvious: it ingeniously unites the twin poles of his belief, Classicism and Christianity. On the origin of the orders few genuinely new contributions, however speculative, have been made since Vitruvius. Yet for someone so deeply English in instincts and preferences, it may seem ironic that Terry's thought should belong to a tradition of radical inquiry which is essentially French: a fact that was reflected in the essay's having won a distinguished French prize.

As was suggested in Chapter 1, Terry's religion and his Classicism also coincide in

1. Since writing this Terry says that he has found additional corroboration of his theories in Velikowski's *World in Chaos.*

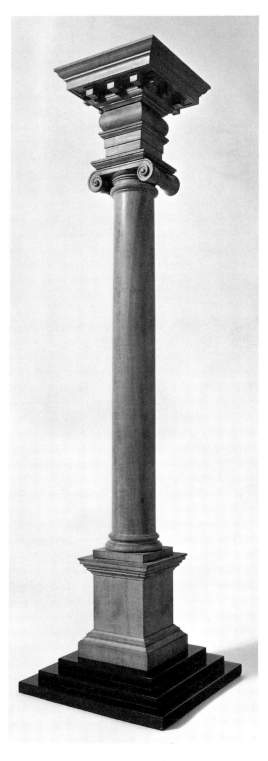

179. Ionic order

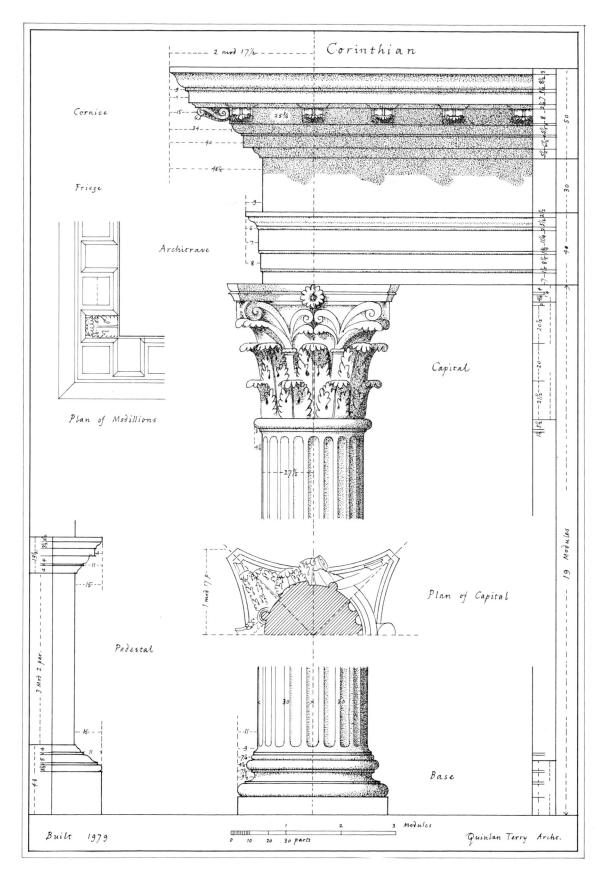

Corinthian

Cornice

Frieze

Architrave

Capital

Plan of Modillions

Pedestal

Plan of Capital

Base

Built 1979

0   10   20   30 parts

1   2   3 Modules

Quinlan Terry Archs.

180. Corinthian order

a more general way. His belief in the God of order is reflected in an architecture of order, in which peace, harmony, quietness, rightness and simplicity are the dominant characteristics. He has none of Francis Johnson's fondness for surprises: his plans do not create unexpected contrasts of space or scale. Thus, in the lecture 'Genuine Classicism' he defines the true qualities of a Classical building in the following terms:

i. The plan is symmetrical, albeit with slight variations. ii. The front door is in the middle. iii. The windows are about right in size and shape and come in the right place. iv. The roof is pitched and simple. v. The materials are traditional. vi. The walls that you see are solid and loadbearing, carrying the roof and floor. vii. The proportions of the house are expressed by one of the Classical orders. The proportion of the ground floor is often expressed in a smaller order around the front door.

We have seen these commonsense criteria in the buildings discussed throughout this book. Terry's object in stating them is to forestall any confusion about definitions. In recent years Classicism has become to architecture what democracy is to politics: a slogan that nearly everyone, of whatever persuasion, feels entitled to brandish, and which can accordingly mean everything or nothing depending on who is laying claim to it. 'The common man has no doubt in his mind what classicism means,' Terry said in a speech to the Architecture Club before the Prince of Wales on 13 February 1985. 'It means columns and capitals and cornices; it means pediments and pilasters and pinnacles; it means architraves and arches

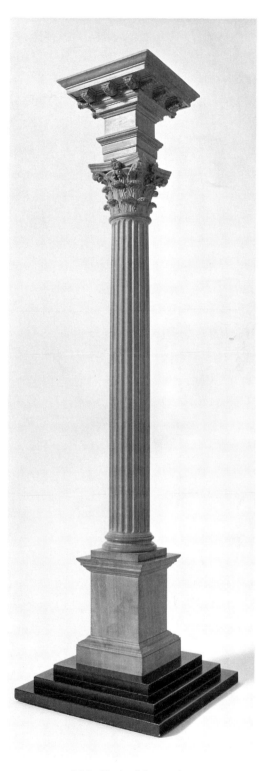

181. Corinthian order

185

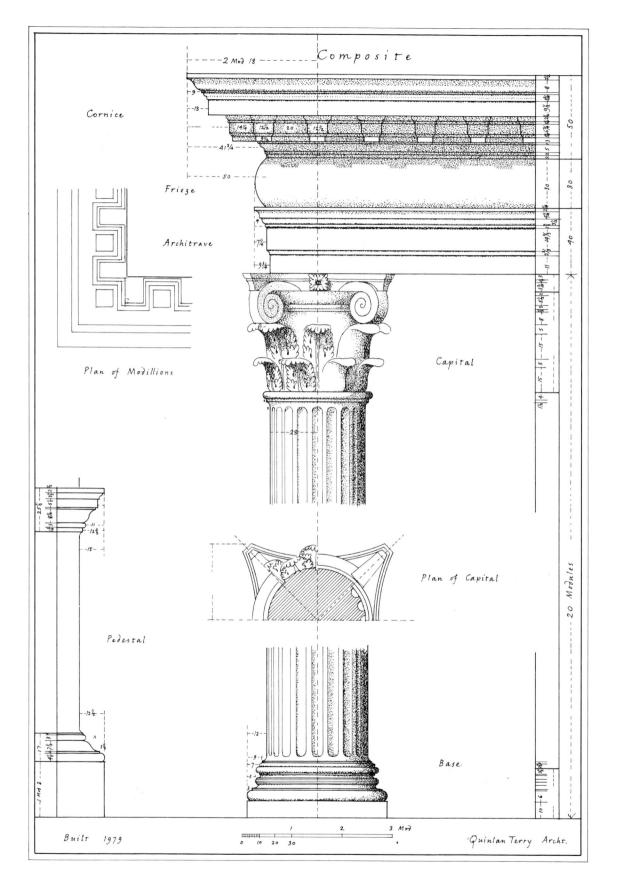

Composite

Cornice

Frieze

Architrave

Plan of Modillions

Capital

Plan of Capital

Pedestal

Base

20 Modules

Built 1979

Quinlan Terry Archt.

182. Composite order

and archivolts. But the expert would say no, it means clean lines, it means a rational disposition of parts, or mental discipline or grain and texture; quite forgetting that all the classical architects of the past employed the orders, Tuscan, Doric, Ionic, Corinthian and Composite ...'

But despite this Terry's seven criteria of Classicism are not quite about Classicism and nothing else. Classicism is a style in the same way that we can now see that the Modern Movement was a style: it is no less legitimate to build a temple with a fibreglass finial, in imitation of stone, than it was to build the Bauhaus out of brick coated with cement, in imitation of concrete. Nevertheless, we have seen that Terry was an Arts and Crafts man before he was a Classicist and this has affected his attitude to what can be called simply, 'sound building'. Dufours Place is not articulated by an order, except the small one flanking the front door, but it *is* built of a traditional material, load-bearing brick (which with its mortar has a pleasing texture and colour), and in such a way that it will not easily fall down. This is of some interest to the client; it also allows the architect to sleep peacefully at night, since he knows he will not be dragged through the liability courts.

Modern materials (Portland cement concrete, steel, reinforced concrete, reconstructed stone, precast concrete, sandlime bricks, stainless steel, aluminium, laminated plastics) generally have a shorter life than their traditional equivalents (lime-

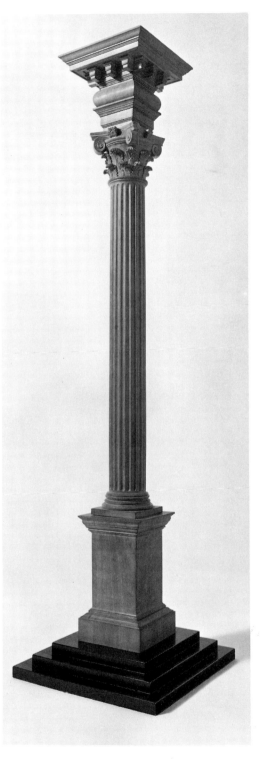

183. Composite order

187

stone, marble, lime concrete, clay bricks and tiles, slates, sandstone and timber).[2] Terry is 'no obscurantist': he has on one occasion or another used most forms of modern material but only for short-term cheapness and in particular circumstances (which I have endeavoured to describe throughout the book). He accepts that modern materials 'have their uses for temporary buildings like exhibition halls and factories'. But all too often the short-term expediency of using modern materials is, with the years, overwhelmed by drawbacks that only make themselves known after building has finished.

The symbol of wrong-headed building methods is Portland cement concrete, particularly when it is reinforced. It is just acceptable, perhaps, when it is not exposed to the weather (and has been used by Terry where it is not necessary for the structure to last beyond a certain period) but never when there is the slightest possibility that water may penetrate. The point is not merely that, as a facing, it invariably stains. Evidence of the latent dangers of this material appear in the newspapers almost daily. It may not always be fallible. But Terry's belief is that in our imperfect world it can never be one hundred per cent reliable, and any margin for error, however small, could lead to tragedy – if only for the architect, faced with litigation and exorbitant costs being awarded against him.

Reinforced concrete is both unsatisfactory in itself and unsanctioned by tradition. It is unsatisfactory for three reasons. Firstly, because dense concretes are subject to a far higher degree of thermal movement than all traditional materials – for instance limestones (0.12in as against 0.03–0.04in on a ten foot length through 160° temperature difference, according to the Building Research Station Digest no.99). In other words it expands in the sun and contracts in the cold. To allow for this it is necessary to set expansion joints at frequent intervals in any large concrete structure: these expansion joints are filled with a soft mastic to take up the movement. The problem comes when, in the course of time, the mastic fails or becomes clogged with pebbles and other material, with the result that movement is no longer possible and the concrete cracks.

Secondly, if water penetrates, the reinforcement in the concrete is liable to rust; once the rust has started it spreads rapidly down the length of the steel bar. While decay in traditional building materials manifest itself gradually and can be seen by the naked eye, a rusting reinforcement bar is hidden from view. Often the first that is known of it is when it gives out completely and that section of the building collapses. Firemen are reluctant to fight fires for as long in concrete-framed

2. See 'Seven Misunderstandings about Classical Architecture' in the catalogue of the 1981 Quinlan Terry exhibition at Academy Editions.

buildings as in those traditionally constructed, because the floors, when they go, collapse suddenly without warning.

Thirdly, reinforced concrete demands a high degree of technology in the construction. This is largely a technology that the site foreman does not naturally understand: he builds according to someone else's specifications, without knowledge of his own. It is therefore not obvious to him if a faulty calculation has crept in. If a nought too few or too many appears in the specifications for a building of bricks and mortar, it is all too obvious to the tradesmen concerned: they stop work and phone the architect for clarification.

To Terry, the overwhelming argument in favour of traditional materials is precisely that they have the accumulated experience of a tradition behind them. 'We are told that Physick was invented in a thousand years by a thousand thousand men,' he wrote in the Kingswalden Notes. 'It is the same with architecture. Therefore to ignore tradition is childish, but to do the opposite, like the moderns, is ... words fail me. I think it must be the product of a diseased mind!' However extensively the manufacturer may test a new product, it must remain an all but unknown commodity in relation to materials that have been in use for many centuries.

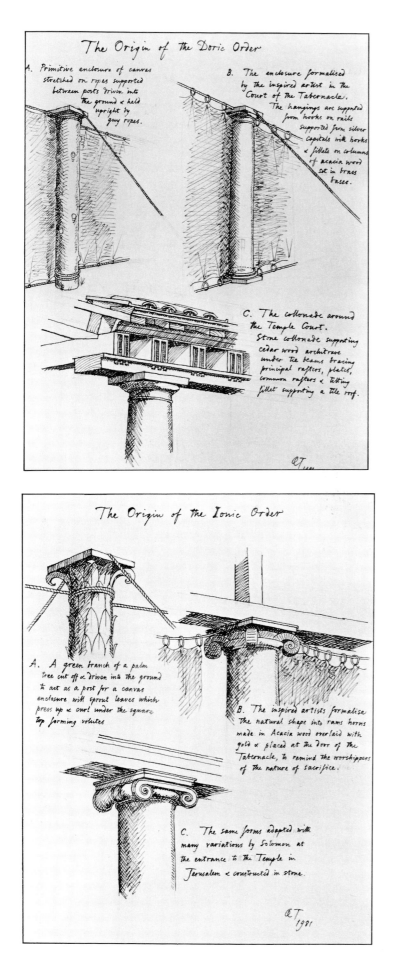

The Origin of the Doric Order

A. Primitive enclosure of canvas stretched on ropes supported between posts driven into the ground & held upright by guy ropes.

B. The enclosure formalised by the inspired artist in the Court of the Tabernacle. The hangings are supported from hooks on rails supported from silver capitals with hooks & fillets on columns of acacia wood set in brass bases.

C. The colonnade around the Temple Court. Stone colonnade supporting cedar wood architrave under tie beams bracing principal rafters, plates, common rafters & tilting fillet supporting a tile roof.

The Origin of the Ionic Order

A. A green branch of a palm tree cut off & driven into the ground to act as a post for a canvas enclosure with sprout leaves which press up & curl under the square top forming volutes

B. The inspired artists formalise the natural shape into rams horns made in Acacia wood overlaid with gold & placed at the door of the Tabernacle, to remind the worshippers of the nature of sacrifice.

C. The same forms adapted with many variations by Solomon at the entrance to the Temple in Jerusalem & constructed in stone.

184. Origin of the Doric order

185. Origin of the Ionic order

186. Origin of the Corinthian order (facing)

187. Orders to the same scale

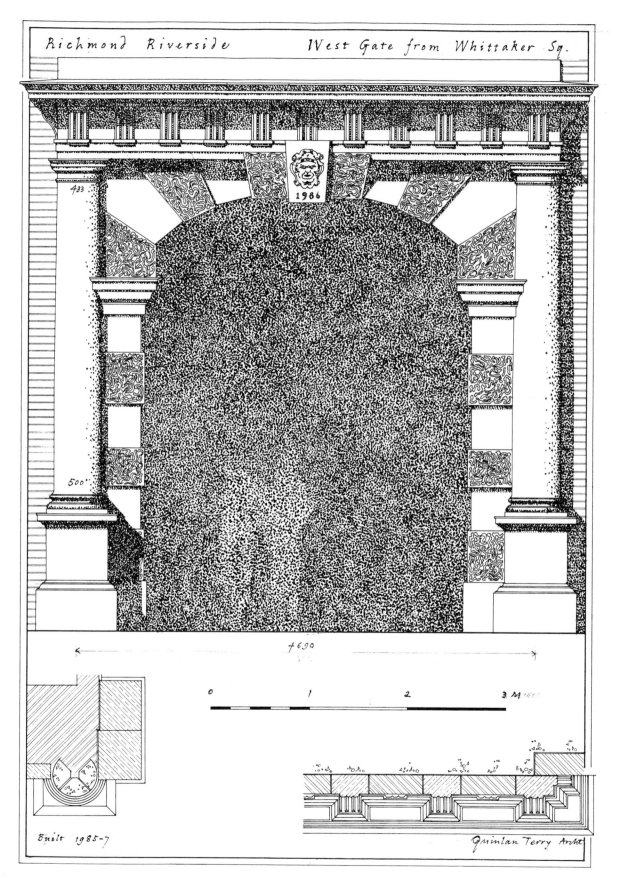

188. Richmond Riverside: West Gate from Whittaker Square

CHAPTER TWELVE

RICHMOND RIVERSIDE AND DOWNING

The modern speculative office block has become to many people the pre-eminent symbol of capitalism run amok, gobbling up Britain's cities. Through its overbearing scale and use of the alien materials discussed in the last chapter, it is a focus for the widespread public disenchantment with post-war architecture – expressed in the outcry against the proposed Mies van der Rohe tower by the Mansion House. Terry's principal achievement may be to show that this bad image – bad for the public who are forced to suffer the buildings, bad for the employees who work in them, bad for the reputation of the firms which pay the rent – is not inescapable. He is fortunate in working with a developer, Haslemere Estates, which is not only sympathetic to a more humane architectural approach but which, crucially, has responded quickly to the need for smaller office units. The benefits will be seen in the Richmond Riverside development immediately to the north and west of Richmond Bridge, which was started in March 1985 and is due for completion in July 1987. Richmond Riverside is Terry's first opportunity to apply Classicism on a large scale to a major urban site.

It is a site that had over the years become hideously snagged in the machinery of planning. A series of developers and their architects had attempted to extricate it, and had themselves become enmeshed. Before Haslemere the most recent had been the English Property Corporation, who employed the architects Brewer, Smith and Brewer. Alas for them, their scheme was thirteen years in grinding through the mill. One suspects that the long agony dimmed some of the architects' original enthusiasm, for their final designs were a peculiarly lacklustre compromise between Modern and the Georgian style with which Richmond is identified. The interest here lies in the brief. In the hope of attracting big corporate users, EPC wished the office accommodation over the whole site (some 109,000 square feet) to be capable of letting as one or at most two big units. The planners insisted on some effort at diversity, appropriate to the slope of the site and the character of the area. Floor levels had to continue through what appeared to be separate buildings. Brick was used, but as a veneer on a concrete frame. Finally EPC obtained planning permission from Richmond Borough Council, but decided not to see the scheme through.

Enter Haslemere. They agreed to buy the site on condition that their scheme, designed by Terry, was approved. Terry's drawings were very different. Rather than producing one vast building which tried to give the impression of being subdivided, he has treated the site as a series of attached but separate houses, with party walls. So each building is what it seems: a separate architectural entity. The separateness has been reinforced by the style. For at Richmond Terry has developed Erith's joke of instant history and the Picturesque contrasts of Frog Meadow and the Baha'i temple. Each separate building is in a different Classical manner – whether that of Chambers, Palladio, Venetian Gothic, the Baroque or the Greek Revival. This is only possible because Haslemere, while keeping approximately the same floor area as EPC, have decided that small is beautiful and will let the fifteen separate buildings on the site as several different units. They believe that, at a time when London is overstocked with speculative office accommodation, there is still a big demand for middle-sized premises. Haslemere is going into the project with the Pension Fund Property Unit Trust, but unlike many institutional investors they together have the flexibility to think in terms other than those of single monolithic developments.

As always, Terry liked to begin designing from the given conditions of the task: these were the existing planning consent obtained by EPC, the slope of the ground and the desire to preserve certain listed and unlisted buildings in what is a conservation area. It is one of the skills of any capable architect to turn constraints into assets and this is precisely what Terry has done. He has evolved an architectural form that is pleasing to his own penchant for eclecticism, wholly appropriate to Richmond and seductive to public taste. When, in December 1983, the Council mounted an exhibition to consult the public about the EPC and Haslemere schemes, a majority of 900 to 150 of those who returned questionnaires preferred Haslemere's.

Seductive: some will say too seductive. The precedent for treating a continuous run of buildings in one development in a number of contrasting styles must be Nash's Regent Street; but one suspects that, inevitably, critics who are not Terry fans will attempt to denigrate the Richmond Riverside scheme by calling it Portmeirion or even 'Quality Street'. They will be wrong. Richmond Riverside is

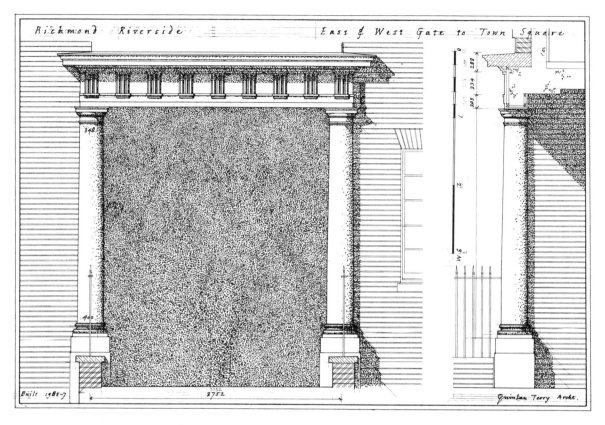

189. Richmond Riverside: East and West Gate to Town Square

not a stage set – the buildings are real, with load-bearing walls – and, given that the buildings will be occupied by different owners, it is absolutely reasonable to treat them in different styles. A massive, unified Classical statement was in any case ruled out by the site: it not only slopes upwards from the bridge but, from the top of Bridge Street, downwards along Hill Street. Much highly expensive levelling of the ground would have been necessary to attempt an Escorial or even a Somerset House. Also, on Bridge Street and Hill Street it is not possible to step back and take in the whole length of one façade. What is more, there was a planning requirement that certain key features were retained. These principally comprised three houses in the terrace fronting the river: Henry Laxton's Italianate Tower House of 1856 on the corner by the bridge, Palm Court (also of the 1850s) and Heron House, a listed building dated 1716. In addition Haslemere felt that the Town Hall by W. J. Ancell of 1893 was too good to lose, particularly because of the entrance, grand staircase and the main Council Chamber, all of which will be restored. The conservation of these buildings both precluded a comprehensive scheme and argued in favour of one divided up into smaller masses, which would not dwarf the existing structures. So if the solution adopted was not exactly forced on Terry, it was at least perfectly logical for him to take it. And of course there is no denying that it happens also to fall in with his eagerness always to experiment with ideas from his sketchbooks or sourcebooks that he has not tried before.

The perimeter of the site is formed by three streets – Bridge Street, Hill Street and Water Lane – and the river. Let us look first at the vitally important river elevation, starting with Tower House – a quite undistinguished but lovable riverside villa, with its campanile and three-sided window bay (on the far right of Figure 196). The interior of Tower House is being altered to include a two-floor restaurant with access to the terrace above the boathouse on the towpath. To the left comes Palm Court, and then, in place of a thin and indifferent 1930s insertion, a new pedimented building. This will provide a gateway cribbed from Palladio's Basilica at Vicenza through to Town Square behind – the Palladian motif being repeated in the two upper storeys. To the left again comes Heron House, with a flat front of five bays; and at the end of the terrace will be a new, eleven-bay building called Hotham House, with a pediment, stucco quoins and rustication. Like Merks Hall, the end elevation of Hotham House has a seventeenth-century feeling, with a double-sweep of steps, pediment, widow's walk and cupola – though a suggestion of Roman Baroque creeps into the first-floor window surround.

At this point you come to Whittaker Square. The Brewer, Smith and Brewer scheme had been designed loosely around a number of courtyards. To Terry the site also indicated a courtyard theme but he made his more formal, like those of Oxford or Cambridge colleges or the Inns of Court. In Terry's scheme there will be three squares – Town Square, Whittaker Square and Castle Square – and a service yard enclosed on three sides. Whittaker Square is the only one to be roughly square in shape. It will be open on the south-west side to the river, with a flight of shallow rising pony steps – like those of the Spanish Steps in Rome, for example – aligned on the war memorial to lead down to the towpath. On either side of the steps will be a zigzag pattern of paths. Typically, the starting point for this satisfying piece of geometry was the requirement to provide wheelchair ramps for disabled access. These ramps are carried through in paths towards Bridge Street. So from the other side of the bridge you will see a formal terraced lawn with trees and bushes in front of a terrace of old and new Classical buildings – with, standing forward on the extreme left, a restaurant with two (on the river three) superimposed arcades: its happy, Venetian flavour appropriate to its

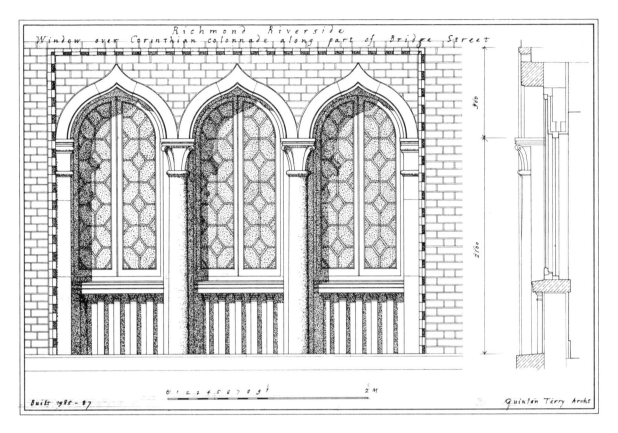

190. Richmond Riverside: windows over Corinthian colonnade, Bridge Street

riverside position. The Doric and Ionic arcades were derived from Palladio's Convento della Carità.

This is as it were the scheme's garden front. For the street elevations you might return to Tower House and begin walking up Bridge Street. If you wish, you may do so under cover, for a continuous colonnade runs all the way round the Bridge Street and Hill Street fronts. After Tower House the three buildings in the Bridge Street terrace are all new. The materials are traditional, and each building is in a different Classical idiom. First comes the biggest of the group: built of Mulberry stock bricks with an arched and rusticated lower storey. The central feature has two superimposed Palladian windows and stone quoins, and is appropriately assertive, for it incorporates one of the entrances to Town Square. And a massive entrance it is, very wide and tall and flanked by blocked Roman Doric columns and pilasters. The drama of this is reminiscent of Bartolommeo Ammanati's court-yard of the Pitti Palace. Perhaps, too, one can taste something of the Belgian College in Rome which Terry measured for the Roman Sketchbook. But once

197

again the idea had its origin in a purely practical necessity, that of providing a four metre by three metre access for fire engines. The big opening required a big span, which in turn suggested bold voussoirs. These set the scene for rustication, while the need, physically and visually, to lighten the burden above a flat arch indicated the Palladian windows. Remember this Doric entrance, because it provides a theme that will recur in Town Square.

Next on Bridge Street is the most capricious, or capriccio-like, note in the scheme: a four-bay building that, Terry hopes, will recall the back streets of Venice, particularly those streets where the original builders ran out of steam towards the top and ended with a plain attic and simple, typically Venetian cornice. The capitals to the colonnade are Corinthian but debased, having been modelled on ones on the Palazzo Venezia in Rome. On the first and second floor the windows are ogee-headed, with keystones sweeping upwards in a quiff (because the shape is created out of the keystone, the arch is not weakened). As in Venice, the windows have polygonal lead glazing bars.

At the top of Bridge Street, the building on the corner is new, but at the ground floor commemorates the attractive jeweller's, Jarvis, that was there before. The planners' input into the design of the scheme has been relatively slight, but one point that did cause Terry an adjustment was their observation that the cupola originally intended for this building was too large. It was found that it was possible to reduce the size. This cupola, like the others throughout the scheme, is more than a frivolous ornament, since it conceals the extract from the basement car park and duct work to the air-conditioning plant.

Turning down Hill Street, the most striking front is that of the long Greek Revival building, which looks as though it could be a corn exchange in a provincial town. The baseless Doric colonnade had already been tried in the Turban Development at Woodbridge, where Terry was commissioned to redesign the front of a shopping complex which had failed to win planning approval. This was on a similar sloping site and the baseless order was chosen so that the column heights could be steadily increased down the gradient. On the other side of a five-bay building, with rusticated arches on the ground floor and a Diocletian window in the attic, comes another long building – seven bays – in Tuscan. The finials are like those that Terry previously proposed for a gateway for David McAlpine, which the client rejected. At the end is the florid town hall. Terry does not resent the retention of the existing buildings: he feels that they offer 'another colour in the artist's palette'.

Not having the excuse of fire engines, Hill Street's entrance to Town Square is

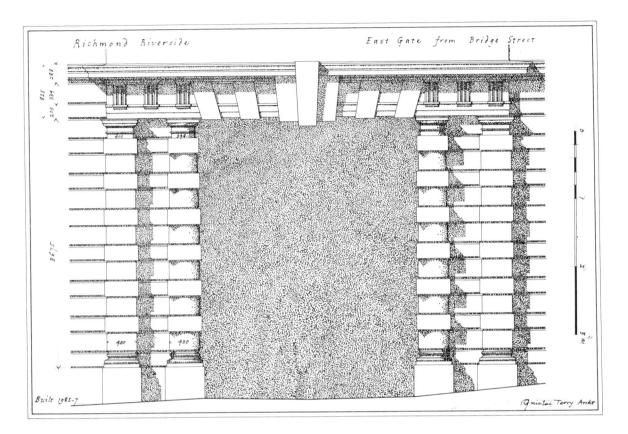

191. Richmond Riverside: East Gate from Bridge Street

undemonstrative. It lies in the centre of the Greek Doric section of the colonnade, and is aligned on the gateway to the river on the opposite side of the square and, it was ultimately decided, on the fountain. (Originally it was thought to be more intriguing that one should first see the fountain from an angle.) Let us go through to Town Square. It has the sense of repose and harmony that is so important to Terry's life and work. As Terry wrote in the text accompanying the 1983 Richmond Riverside exhibition: 'Town Square is to be one of those spaces where simple architecture surrounds a pleasant garden; quiet for work inside or recreation outside.' As you stand beneath the arch from Hill Street and look around you, the buildings to either side look solid, decent, dignified. They are mostly in brick, but looking back at the building you have just passed through, fronting Hill Street, you see that it has a rusticated centrepiece and end bays, and that the arch has coupled Ionic columns to either side. Glancing diagonally across to the left, you may notice a broad opening with a Doric order supporting an entablature. This is the other side of the dramatic Doric entrance from Bridge Street. Doric having been established as the signature tune, it is carried through on this axis across the square. Opposite the Bridge Street entrance the way through to Whittaker Square – a longish tunnel, but wide enough for the fire engines – again has a Doric order, again with a Palladian window above, although here the window to the second floor has a deliciously debased surround, with ears to top and bottom and misplaced guttae (which belong in the Doric frieze) appended in the eighteenth-century Roman manner beneath. It is on the other side of this building, however, that the richest variation is played on the Doric theme. Town Square itself slopes slightly to the north-west, and this gradient continues more steeply towards Whittaker Square, with the result that the ground level of the Whittaker Square entrance is several feet lower than that from Bridge Street. But Terry has kept his Doric columns at the same level throughout: this has meant giving them bases on both the Town Square entrance to Whittaker Square and vice-versa. And because the Whittaker Square entrance is lower it is also taller, giving sufficient room for an impost (in fact the capital of a squat Tuscan order) and arch. The voussoirs and blocks to the pilaster have been vermiculated.

We cannot leave Town Square without noticing the 'parterres' created by patterning of granite setts. These in fact cover a reinforced concrete raft that forms the roof to the car park underground. Terry would have preferred not to have used this material, but the alternative of brick vaulting – though marvellous in its possibilities for drama – would not have allowed enough car parking spaces. The raft, however, has no contact with the buildings, and it has been a tricky problem how to incorporate an expansion joint into the pavement region without giving undue offence to the eye.

From the Whittaker Square entrance the view across Whittaker Square is entirely taken up by The Castle, the long, handsome range that is the biggest building in the development. The name perpetuates that of the Castle Hotel, a poor piece of the William IV period, which was Classical but asymmetrical and shocked Terry, as he wrote in the Richmond exhibition, by its solecism of 'a superimposed order with a central pilaster'. The new Castle is based on Chambers's fourth scheme for Richmond Palace: it is both better architecture and allows more office space. Above a rusticated ground floor it has a centrepiece with a pediment and attached Corinthian columns and end pavilions with pilasters. In contrast to Chambers's design the entrance lies at ground level: it would have been impractical to have had it on the first floor with a grand flight of steps up to the piano nobile. The plan of The Castle is simple, showing how well a building of this kind works for modern needs. It has an impressive entrance hall with a

200

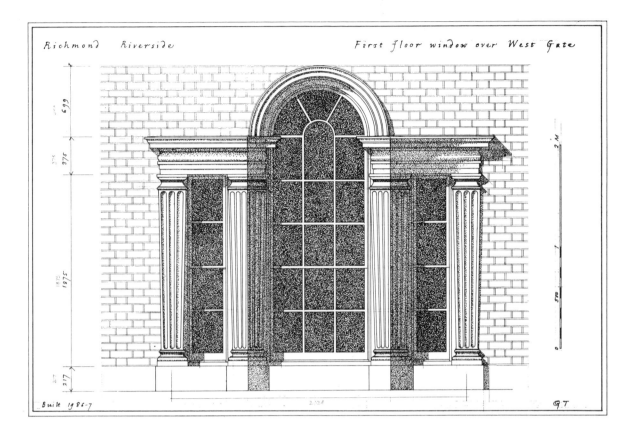

192. Richmond Riverside: window over West Gate

staircase and large open-plan offices to either side, with second fire-escape stair-cases at either end.

Your tour of Richmond Riverside finishes when you walk through The Castle and out by the door to Castle Square. The body of this square is almost triangular, but at the top it steps back in two wedges formed by the boundaries of the old Gaumont Cinema site. On the side facing Water Lane are twenty-three flats, arranged in two brick and sash-windowed blocks connected by a burst of flint-faced Gothick in the form of a castellated tower. The accommodation here, at the quietest end of the site, is as dignified and peaceful as one would expect in this Borough.

193. Downing College: east door

DOWNING COLLEGE: THE NEW HOWARD BUILDING

The new Howard Building for Downing College, Cambridge, is a happy note to end on: happy because it is intended as a 'villa of pleasure', and happy too because, like a country house, it is more a piece of pure architecture, where the object in view is a beautiful building, than a hard profit and loss calculation. It also stands as a happy, if rare, emblem of the ways in which academic learning can be of practical benefit to both the world at large and the college in particular. For this ornament to Downing is the gift of the Howard Foundation, established by Dr Alan Howard, a member of the college, from the royalties from his internationally successful Cambridge Diet, developed at the University Department of Medicine. And to some there may yet be one further sense in which the commission is happy, as it shows Terry, severest of low churchmen though he be, giving his bent for architectural flamboyance full rein.

It is even possible that Terry felt that Wilkins's chaste Greek Doric had cast too

202

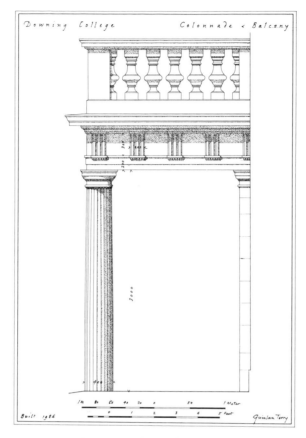

194. Downing College: porch

much of a chill on the atmosphere. Architecturally, the Howard Building warms the college up; and if Phase Two is completed it will also give Downing what, through the lack of funds to carry through the original scheme, it has never had: the quintessentially Cambridge sense of buildings round an enclosed court. The Howard Building stands at the north end of the West Lodge garden, which already has buildings on two sides and trees on a third. Its neighbours will be Edward Barry's West Range of 1873 and Sir Herbert Baker's North Range of 1930 – each subdued by the proximity of Wilkins, each looking in need of a bit of go. And go is exactly what the Howard Building will give them – though still within the bounds of harmony.

For the flamboyance comes in the details. As so often in Terry's work, the basic shape of the building, which is of Ketton and Portland stone, is four-square. Indeed, the principal requirement of a room to seat two hundred people for lectures and plays made his first thoughts remember the church hall of St Mary's, Paddington Green. But at Downing this big room was to be on the first floor – the

203

195. *Downing College: Howard Building, elevation*

piano nobile – which indicated staircases for fire escapes at each end. Unlike the more utilitarian church hall, however, the lecture theatre will be articulated with Ionic pilasters, to give a good bit of architecture to rest the eyes on during moments of longeur. It will also have an open timber queen post roof as in the early Christian basilicas: this has the practical benefit of giving somewhere to hang the lighting gear, but was really done to show that this is, as Terry puts it, 'a genuine piece of building'. The building is entered at ground-floor level, where there is a foyer and bar. Initially the basement was conceived as a big room for discos; to minimize noise it was to have had no windows, and this had a design implication, since the air-conditioning extractors required small turrets at either end of the roof. Later it was decided to omit the basement on grounds of cost.

As work on the design went on, the idea of St Mary's church hall became increasingly married to that of the Heseltines' summerhouse. Like the summer-house, the Howard Building has a giant Corinthian order of unequally spaced columns and pilasters, with a niche set amid rustication in the bays at either end. There is a pediment with finials and a barn-like slate roof. A window appearing unexpectedly just below the cornice expresses the mezzanine floor containing the slide projection room and motor room for the main hall.

The building is a pleasure pavilion to be used, at least in part, as a theatre: this is reflected in the main entrance on the north front. It is Doric, but the orders are overlapped by a swirling cartouche of stone – 'lubricious,' says Terry, 'I think I found it in Spain' – which suggests the parting of curtains before the performance begins. Despite the ripeness of the curves, the effect has a Mannerist quality from being in two dimensions rather than three, which is a minor hallmark of Terry's work. The Doric order, however, is carried through the building and out into the colonnade supporting the balcony to the lecture theatre on the south; and the order also emerges in the doorcases to north and south. Phase Two will be a residential block which will complete the court, with a colonnade that will unite it with the other buildings.

Terry believes that Downing is his best building to date. The question, for a man with every prospect of twenty years of practice to come, remains only: where next?

Hotham House

1 : 50 Scale

198. Richmond Riverside: river front

196. Bridge Street elevation

197. Richmond Riverside: Hill Street elevation

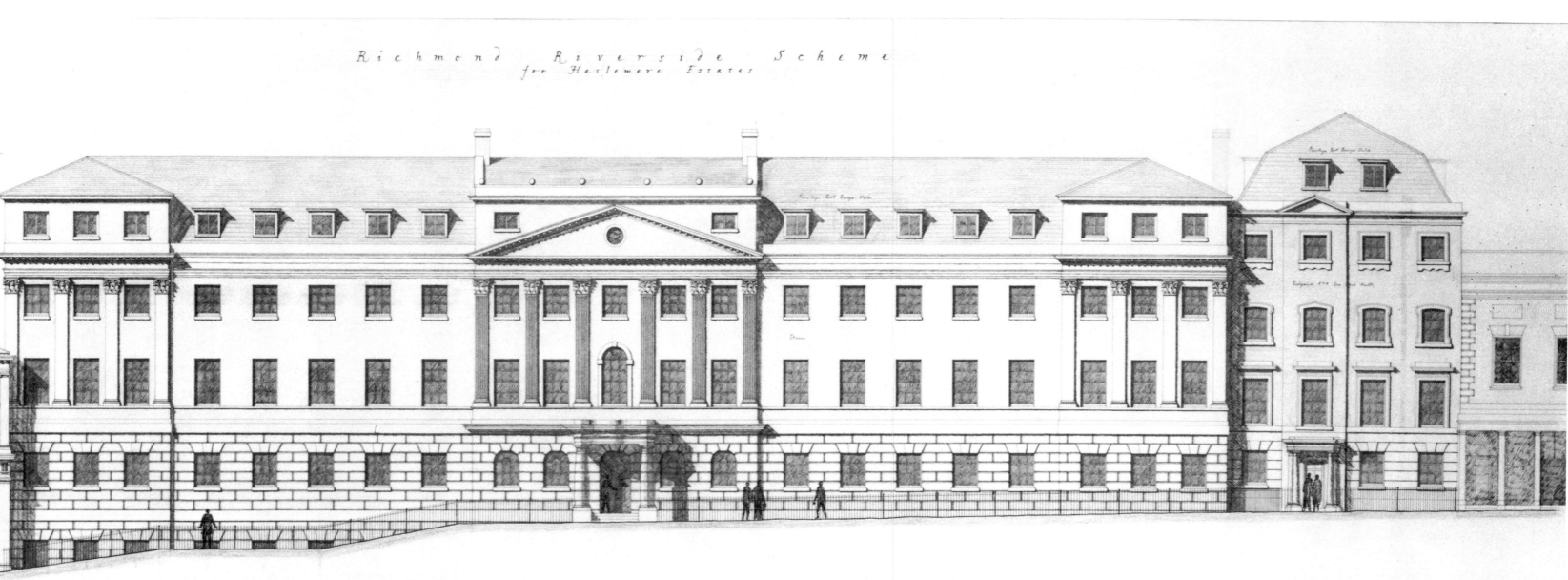

Richmond Riverside Scheme
for Haslemere Estates

The Castle

Office 10

POSTSCRIPT

THE REVOLUTION COMPLETED

Offices and new buildings for Oxbridge colleges: both Richmond Riverside and the Howard Building belong to building types that until recently seemed the strongest bastions of Modernism. The wheel of taste has spun so fast that now a Classical solution in both cases seems nothing less than natural. It was equally natural for the owner of Merks Hall to destroy a house put up in 1961 because it was ugly and inefficient and to put a proper building in its place. It was natural for an insurance company to invest in a two-hundred-year-old warehouse, which has another two hundred years of life left in the fabric, because the warehouse was built before architecture had started to go wrong. Not surprisingly perhaps, the course taken by his practice in the last few years has convinced Terry that the revolution begun by the Modern Movement has been completed: that the wheel has gone on turning, bringing us back to the point at which we began. The Modern Movement set the world on its head. We are now standing on our feet again. It is as though the Modern Movement had not happened.

Well, it is a dream; but one that may yet come true. Those who have an evolutionist view of history will say that it is always necessary to build on the past, to move forward from the last place we reached. But Terry is not an evolutionist, in this sense or in others. He believes that if mankind has gone astray, it should repent. Years ago architecture wandered off the right path and got itself hopelessly lost. The only thing to do is to return to the path. It is the same path as before. For him it is the sole path.

'Two wrongs don't make a right,' as Terry's associate, Hugh Barrell, would say. Or in Terry's language, only one path leads to the Heavenly City.

OFFICE LIST OF WORKS SINCE 1973

This list includes only work that was built. It is arranged by the year in which the jobs came into the office.

1973

ST MARY'S CHURCH, PADDINGTON GREEN, LONDON. Site works, railings and gates.

WESTGATE HOUSE, DEDHAM, ESSEX. For Christopher Davies, Esq. Addition.

DEVEREUX FARM, KIRBY-LE-SOKEN, ESSEX. For J.W. Eagle, Esq. Addition.

CRAIG-Y-BWLA, CRICKHOWELL, POWYS. For George Williams, Esq. New bridge and summerhouse.

BROOK HOUSE, WALSHAM-LE-WILLOWS, SUFFOLK. For Lord Cayzer. Alterations, restoration and garden seats.

HOUBRIDGE HALL, GREAT OAKLEY, ESSEX. For E.B. Cooper, Esq. Re-roofing.

SPRING FARM, WIX, ESSEX. For J.A.R. Cooper, Esq. Re-roofing.

1974

ST MARY'S CHURCH, PADDINGTON GREEN, LONDON. New organ and case.

WEST WYCOMBE, BUCKINGHAMSHIRE. For Sir Francis Dashwood Bt. New cricket pavilion.

THE PEDIMENT, AYNHO, NORTHAMPTONSHIRE. For Miss Elizabeth Watt. Miscellaneous works.

OLD HALL FARM, HEMINGSTONE, SUFFOLK. For Dan Neuteboom, Esq. New addition.

NO.1 HIGH STREET, DEDHAM, ESSEX. For Mrs Raymond Erith. Repairs.

1 ALWYNE VILLAS, CANONBURY, LONDON. For Mr and Mrs John Salusbury. New addition.

ARCHENDINES FARMHOUSE, FORDHAM, CAMBRIDGESHIRE. For Arthur Evans, Esq. New flat.

BELL COTTAGE, DEDHAM, ESSEX. For L.H. Thomas, Esq. Restoration.

1975

WEST GREEN HOUSE, HAMPSHIRE. For Lord McAlpine of West Green. New column, nymphaeum, bridge, grotto, seat, Doric lodge, birdcage, and other garden works.

QUINLAN TERRY

ST JOHN'S CHURCH, GREAT HORKESLEY, ESSEX. New addition.

DORKING TYE HOUSE, BURES, ESSEX. For Ian Swan, Esq. Restoration and extension.

GOLDENFERRY FARM, WIX, ESSEX. For J.A.R. Cooper, Esq. Re-roofing and general repairs.

1976

CHARLTON, OXFORDSHIRE. Tombstone of the 2nd Earl of Birkenhead.

OLD COTTAGE, BRADENHAM, BUCKINGHAMSHIRE. For the National Trust. Alterations.

OLD RECTORY, LAMARSH, SUFFOLK. For D.M. Anderson, Esq. Extension and garden work.

ST MARY'S CHURCH, PADDINGTON GREEN, LONDON. New church hall.

ST PANCRAS OLD CHURCH, LONDON. Restoration.

NETHER HALL, BRADFIELD , ESSEX. For the Hon. Richard Seebohm. Repairs.

BROOK COTTAGES, DEDHAM, ESSEX. For Mrs Raymond Erith. Restoration.

THATCH COTTAGE, WIX, ESSEX. For J.A.R. Cooper, Esq. New Addition.

1977

WAVERTON HOUSE, NEAR MORETON-IN-MARSH, GLOUCESTERSHIRE. For Mr and Mrs Jocelyn Hambro. New house.

NO. 4 FROG MEADOW, DEDHAM, ESSEX. For B.R.Winch, Esq. New house.

SPEARINGS SHOP, DEDHAM, ESSEX. New side door.

LITTLE MISSENDEN CHURCH, BUCKINGHAMSHIRE. New extension.

THE DOWER HOUSE, LITTLE ROYDON, KENT. For the Hon. David McAlpine. New doorcase. Pope's seat. Fountain and other garden works.

NO.4 CHRISTOPHER ROAD, NORWICH, NORFOLK. For Mr and Mrs John Perowne. Repairs.

ORANGERY AT MAMHEAD, DEVON. For Michael Szell, Esq. Restoration work.

OLD RECTORY, EAST BERGHOLT, SUFFOLK. For Mr and Mrs Rex Cooper. Re-roofing.

1978

HOUSE IN EAST LANE, DEDHAM, ESSEX. For Messrs Baalham and Payne (Builders).

SHERMANS HALL, DEDHAM, ESSEX. For the National Trust. Restoraton and new urn in niche.

BENTLEY FARM, HALLAND, EAST SUSSEX. For Mrs Gerald Askew. New veranda.

WAVERTON STUD, MORETON-IN-MARSH, GLOUCESTERSHIRE. For Mr and Mrs Jocelyn Hambro. New semi-detached cottages.

WORKS

NO.3 BROOK COTTAGES, DEDHAM, ESSEX. For Mrs T. C. Traill. Restoration.

ST PANCRAS OLD CHURCH, LONDON. Restoration Phase II.

1979

NEWFIELD HOUSE, MICKLEY, RIPON, YORKSHIRE. For Mr and Mrs Michael Abrahams. New house.

WEST HILL, COPDOCK, SUFFOLK. For G.F. Harris, Esq. Repairs.

CHEMIST'S SHOP, DEDHAM, ESSEX. For J.Phillips, Esq. Alterations and new addition.

HEWITT HALL, DEDHAM, ESSEX. Classroom extension.

DEDHAM CHURCH, ESSEX. Quinquennial and repairs.

NO.1 SOUTH SQUARE, GRAY'S INN, LONDON. For the Honorable Society of Gray's Inn. Re-building.

NEWTON HOUSE, FRISTON, SUFFOLK. For Mrs C. M. J. Hartley. Restoration.

EAST HOUSE, EAST LANE, DEDHAM, ESSEX. For Mr and Mrs A. W. Regan. Repairs.

CUTLERS GARDENS, LONDON. For Greycoat Estates Ltd. Gate piers and railings.

THE QUEEN'S COLLEGE, OXFORD. Re-decoration of chapel.

ASHFIELD HOUSE, LANGHAM, ESSEX. For Mr and Mrs Drysdale. Restoration and new porch.

NO.14 SOUTH SQUARE, GRAY'S INN, LONDON. For J. A. Kemp, Esq. Alterations.

1980

THE OLD GRAMMAR SCHOOL, DEDHAM, ESSEX. For Michael Ivan, Esq. Restoration.

WELL HOUSE, DEDHAM, ESSEX. For Peter Andrew, Esq. New dormer windows and re-roofing.

THENFORD HOUSE, BANBURY, OXFORDSHIRE. For the Rt Hon. Mr and Mrs Michael Heseltine. New summerhouse. Conversion of outbuildings to estate office and garage.

BENTLEY FARM, HALLAND, EAST SUSSEX. For Mrs Gerald Askew. New trellis arbours.

FAWLEY GREEN, HENLEY-ON-THAMES. For the Hon. David McAlpine. Alterations to hall.

WESTON LODGE, NR BALDOCK, HERTFORDSHIRE. For Mr and Mrs Roderick Pryor. Restoration.

PAVILION AT HATFIELD FOREST. For the National Trust.

SUFFOLK HOUSE, WOODBRIDGE, SUFFOLK. For Mr and Mrs John Strover. Repairs.

WEST WYCOMBE PARK, BUCKINGHAMSHIRE. For Sir Francis Dashwood Bt. New Temple of Venus and grotto.

BROOK HOUSE, HIGH STREET, DEDHAM, ESSEX. For Lord Seebohm. Roof and general repairs.

CROCKLEFORD HALL, ARDLEIGH, ESSEX. For Mrs Kendal. Re-roofing.

1981

STERNFIELD HOUSE, SAXMUNDHAM, SUFFOLK. For Sir Eric and Lady Penn. New clock and maintenance.

BROOKSIDE COTTAGE, GREAT OAKLEY, ESSEX. For E. B. Cooper, Esq. Restoration and repairs.

PRINCEL LANE, DEDHAM, ESSEX. For Messrs Baalham and Payne (Builders). Two new self-contained cottages.

SADDLERS COTTAGE, DEDHAM HEATH, ESSEX. For Mr and Mrs David Dow. Alterations to front elevation.

DUFOURS PLACE and repair and conversion of 48-58 BROADWICK STREET, SOHO, LONDON. For Haslemere Estates.

THE QUEEN'S COLLEGE, OXFORD. Doors to Front and Back Quads. Repairs to pediment and portico to Front Quad.

NOS. 10 and 12 THE GREEN, DUXFORD, CAMBRIDGESHIRE. For Mrs George Glossop.

TURBAN DEVELOPMENT, WOODBRIDGE, SUFFOLK. Restoration of front elevation and new colonnade.

FARNBOROUGH DOWNS FARM, BERKSHIRE. For Mr Adrian and the Hon. Mrs White. New house.

BENGAL HOUSE AND MUSEUM BUILDING, CUTLERS GARDENS, LONDON E1. For the Standard Life Assurance Company. Restoration.

SHRUBS FARM, LAMARSH, SUFFOLK. For Mr and Mrs Robert Erith. Restoration of barn.

BOAT HOUSE, BRIDGES FARM, DEDHAM, ESSEX. For the National Trust. Repairs.

HIGHAM LODGE, HIGHAM, DERBYSHIRE. For Major Gurney. New bookcase and general repairs.

EAST AND WEST SUNNEDON, COGGESHALL, ESSEX. For Miss Rose. Repairs.

1982

THE HERMITAGE, DORSET. For Francis Egerton, Esq. New house.

OLD DEANERY, ST PAUL'S, LONDON. For Haslemere Estates. New gates.

MERKS HALL, GREAT DUNMOW, ESSEX. For Mr and Mrs Richard Wallis. New house.

QUEEN'S COLLEGE, OXFORD. Stone restoration of Back Quad.

WORKS

DEDHAM HALL, DEDHAM, ESSEX. For Mr and Mrs Slingo. Conversion of barn.

RIVERVIEW HOUSE, BRUNDALL, NORWICH, NORFOLK. For Lord Blake. Restoration.

WEST GREEN HOUSE, HAMPSHIRE. For the National Trust. Re-building and repairs following fire damage.

1983

NOS.11, 12 and 13 KENT TERRACE, REGENT'S PARK, LONDON. For Copartnership Property Developments Ltd, part of Rosehaugh plc. Restoration.

DOWNING COLLEGE, CAMBRIDGE. New Howard Building.

RICHMOND RIVERSIDE DEVELOPMENT. For Haslemere Estates.

NETHER HALL, BRADFIELD, ESSEX. For Mr and Mrs S. Bullimore, Repairs and alterations.

LAWFORD HALL, ESSEX. For Mr and Mrs Francis Nichols. Re-roofing. Fountain.

SANDRINGHAM COURT, DUFOURS PLACE, SOHO, LONDON. For Barratt Central London Ltd. Interior of twenty-five luxury flats.

KINGS WALDEN BURY, HERTFORDSHIRE. For Sir Thomas Pilkington Bt. Lightning damage and maintenance.

OLD MILL, SNAPE, SAXMUNDHAM, SUFFOLK. For Mr and Mrs P.J. Terry. Repairs.

HOLLANDS FARM, GREAT OAKLEY, ESSEX. For E.B. Cooper, Esq. Repairs.

EYDON HALL, NORTHAMPTONSHIRE. For Mr and Mrs Gerald Leigh. New stables, garage and courtyards.

WEST WYCOMBE PARK. For Sir Francis Dashwood Bt. New bridge.

1984

NOS.5–8 KENT TERRACE, REGENT'S PARK, LONDON. For Chrysalis Properties Ltd. Restoration.

FARNBOROUGH DOWNS FARM, BERKSHIRE. For Mr Adrian and the Hon. Mrs White. Addition to wing and farm cottage.

THENFORD HOUSE, BANBURY, OXFORDSHIRE. For Mr and Mrs Michael Heseltine. Kitchen garden.

ILLUSTRATION
ACKNOWLEDGEMENTS

The following are thanked for permission to use illustrations: *Country Life* 38, 39, 40, 41 (Alex Starkey); 79, 80, 83,84 (Charles Hall); Mark Fiennes 71; Studio Five 82; *Architects' Journal* (Peter Cook) 155, 156, 157, 158, 159, 160, 161.

All other photographs of buildings are by Charles Hall. The drawings were photographed by Charles Hall and Eileen Tweedy.

SIGNIFICANT PUBLICATIONS
BY QUINLAN TERRY

'Postscript of Roman Sketch Book', 1968. This was translated into German and published in 1981 as part of *In Opposition zur Moderne. Aktuelle Positionen in der Architektur.*

'A Question of Style'. Published by *Architectural Design*, Volume 49 No.3/4, in 1979. It was taken from a lecture given at the RIBA on 21 November 1978. It was later translated into Dutch and published in *Panorama van de avant-garde.*

'Seven Misunderstandings about Classical Architecture'. This was published in the catalogue of the 1981 'Quinlan Terry' exhibition. Translated into French and published by *Archives d'Architecture Moderne*, No.21, 1981. Translated into Dutch and published in *Plan 4/1983*. Translated into Swedish in *Magazin Tessin*.

'One Man's London'. *London Architect*, 1982.

'The Relevance of Neo-Classicism To-day'. The introduction of a lecture published in the catalogue of the Exhibition of Rome Scholars, 1812–82.

'Origins of the Orders'. Essay which won the £5,000 European Prize in 1982 from the Philippe Rotthier Foundation. Translated into French and published by *Archives d'Architecture Moderne*, No. 26, 1984. Published by the *Architectural Review* in February 1983.

'Genuine Classicism'. Lecture given at the RIBA in November 1983. Published in *Transactions* III.

INDEX

INDEX